Manchester and Salford Chartists

Edmund and Ruth Frow

ISBN 0 9523410 4 2

Printed by Lancashire Community Press (TU), 8 Higher Bank Road, Fulwood, Preston PR2 8PD. Tel: (01772) 774756

Contents

Preface

This pamphlet which aims to present recent local research in a popular account, owes much to the painstaking research of Dr Paul A. Pickering. His book, CHARTISM AND THE CHARTISTS IN MANCHESTER AND SALFORD brings to life personalities and places long lost to history. We are very much indebted to him.

Chapter One
Introduction

> Manchester is the seat of the most powerful Unions, the central point of Chartism, the place which numbers the most Socialists. The more the factory system has taken possession of a branch of industry, the more the working men employed in it participate in the Labour Movement.
>
> Frederick Engels[1]

Labour history is too often looked at episodically. Women's Suffrage, Peterloo, the Fight For The Freedom of The Press, each is treated as a specific historical study with a beginning and an end. This is a false picture. The momentous episodes in history arise from the efforts of those who have been active before and continue to influence those who come after. The sharper the conflict between workers and capitalists, the clearer working class consciousness becomes. Chartism was a bewilderingly complex movement with conflicting aims. Arising in the context of its time, it gave birth to the first working class political party in the world and yet never managed to develop a collective leadership.

From the different strands which arose out of the needs of the workers at that time, the NATIONAL CHARTER ASSOCIATION (NCA) attempted to give leadership through many different forms of struggle ranging from peaceful petitioning to armed insurrection. Among the problems which had to be confronted were the relationship between Parliamentary and extra-Parliamentary activity, the role of universal male suffrage, the function of trade unions and of the cooperative movement. The role of the general strike and its relationship to armed insurrection were also on the agenda.

Inevitably, in the immature state of the working class, answers were far from being clear cut. However, Frederick Engels saw the Chartists as "the genuine proletarians all over, the representatives of their class."[2]

Chartism can be conveniently studied under headings:

1 The Emergence of the Movement
2 Manchester in the 1840s.
3 The National Charter Association, Its Organisation and Culture.
4 Chartism and Owenism
5 The General Strike of 1842.
6 1843–1847. A decline in activity and confusion of purpose. Feargus O'Connor's Land Plan.
7 The upsurge in 1848.
8 Chartism in the 1850s.

The roots of Chartism can be traced as far back as the end of the Divine Right of Kings when Charles I lost his head on the scaffold in the 1640s. From that time people claimed access to the Monarch through petitioning. Over the years it had proved a frustrating and ineffectual method of redressing grievances and by the mid-nineteenth century was regarded as futile. The English Revolution had alerted people to the need for a reform of Parliament, but it was the combined influence of the American War of Independence and the French Revolution which had pointed the way to ordinary workers that they had a possible means of gaining some control over their lives.

From the beginning of the century there had been a loose alliance between the rapidly rising middle class and the workers, none of whom had access to the corridors of power. They had no vote and no representatives in a Parliament which only reflected the interests of the landed aristocracy. The 1832 Reform Act enfranchised the wealthier sections of the middle class but the majority of people were ignored. Living and working conditions were atrocious. There was widespread unemployment and rapid technological advances required changes in the relationship between a master and his employees. The Whig Government elected by the first reformed electoral roll in 1832 dismally failed to meet expectations.

Ireland

As soon as "the base, bloody and brutal Whigs"[3] took Office, they showed their determination to ditch all working class aspirations. In the year after their election, they enacted the despotic Irish Coercion Act which gave the military powers to transport or hang Irish men and women without going through the formality of a Court. This provoked an immediate outcry.

In Manchester where many Irishmen had settled in search of work, a vast open air meeting was addressed by John Doherty, leader of the Cotton Spinners' Union who warned the Government that twenty thousand "real, stout, determined Irishmen in the Manchester district were prepared to assist their fellow countrymen to resist the Act"[4] A petition launched at the meeting was presented to Parliament by William Cobbett.[5] It called for withdrawal of the Act, the abolition of Tithes and abandonment of the plan to introduce the hated Poor Law in Ireland. English workers saw in the ferociously repressive regime in Ireland, the blueprint of what the Ruling Class wanted to impose on them.

The Factory Movement

Disillusionment with the Government grew rapidly as it introduced legislation affecting people's lives. In textile factories the Relay System was introduced. This allowed the employer to work one set of children for eight hours followed immediately by another set. It was supposed to protect children from working extended hours, but actually compelled adult workers to work sixteen hours. Moreover the exploitation of children in factories other than textile manufacture, especially in mines, continued. There were no safety regulations and horrific accidents were frequent.

Richard Oastler[6] who was known as The King Of The Factory Children conducted an intensive campaign for a Ten Hour Act in

August, 1832. He and Michael Sadler[7] were invited by Salford and Manchester Short Time Committees to address a joint meeting and to take part in a demonstration. A huge procession with seventeen bands and several hundred banners went to Campfield. A banner at the head of the procession depicted a deformed man asking, AM I NOT A MAN AND A BROTHER? and one of the many contingents of factory children carried a whip and a strap with thongs such as was frequently used on them. Their inscription read, BEHOLD AND WEEP. At Campfield the children joined together to sing their factory song:

We will have the Ten Hours' Bill,
That we will – that we will;
Or the land shall ne'er be still,
We will have the Ten Hours' Bill[8]

Six months later, in May 1833, the children again demonstrated on a Saturday afternoon. They met in St Peter's Field made notorious as the scene of the Peterloo Massacre in 1819. They displayed numerous banners on which were painted portraits of Richard Oastler, Michael Sadler, John Fielding[9] and Lord Ashley[10] all of whom were prominent supporters of the Ten Hours Bill. Other banners bore slogans such as MANUFACTURE WITHOUT CHILD SLAYING and A MUZZLE FOR THE STEAM GIANT. They marched to the York Hotel where the Factory Commissioners appointed to examine working conditions in mills and factories were meeting. A petition asking for shorter hours of work was presented to them.

The New Poor Law

Two years after taking Office, the Whig Government enacted the NEW POOR LAW. The effect was to drive masses of people into destitution. It was described at the time as "The hideous and accurst New Poor Law, which tears asunder the dearest and holiest Ties of Human Heart, which consigns even the Old and Infirm to FAMISH amid the GLOOM and SOLITUDE of a Dungeon Workhouse."[11]

Workers increasingly recognised that the Whig Government had no intention of listening to them or alleviating their conditions in any way. They started a campaign of protest. In Manchester, Christopher Dean,[12] a stonemason, active trade unionist and later a

Chartist, chaired a meeting of the Trades to protest against the new Act. As the campaign developed, fresh activists appeared on the scene. William Willis, an ardent radical and bookseller first appeared as an opponent of the Poor Law. Later he became Secretary of Salford Radical Association.

In March, 1838, R.J. Richardson, William Willis, J.W. Hodgetts,[13] Anton Duxbury[14] and Peter Gendall[15] were elected with Tory support to Salford Select Vestry. When the Tory majority decided a few months later to introduce the Law, the Tory/ Radical alliance was shattered. Attempts to introduce the new regulations in the North of England led in 1837 to a number of clashes. In some places there were street battles, workhouses were pulled down and Poor Law Guardians so terrified that they dare not enforce the Act.

Joseph Raynor Stephens,[16] an expelled Methodist preacher from Stalybridge advocated open and violent defiance. He told a Manchester audience:

> You have no need to fear the power of government, the soldiers, bayonets, and cannon that are all at the disposal of your oppressors; you have a weapon that is far mightier than all these, a weapon against which bayonets and cannon are powerless, and a child of ten years can wield it. You have only to take a couple of matches and a bundle of straw dipped in pitch, and I will see what the Government and its hundreds of thousands of soldiers will do against this one weapon if it is used boldly.[17]

The Unstamped Press

The harsh living and working conditions led many people to question the situation. They wanted answers to problems and sought them through any way that presented itself. Radical journals proliferated. The Government realised that there was a potential danger in such a thirst for knowledge. They imposed a newspaper tax, payment of which had to be displayed on each copy. Henry Hetherington,[18] a radical printer, published THE POOR MAN'S GUARDIAN with the banner headline, "Published in defiance of law to try the power of right against might". The paper was immensely popular and reached many thousands of workers and their families.

Other unstamped periodicals appeared in defiance of the law.

Henry Hetherington

Publishers and vendors were arrested and imprisoned in extremely harsh conditions. But the battle of the unstamped continued.

In Manchester, Abel Heywood had a penny newsroom in Oldham Street. He obtained the agency for THE POOR MAN'S GUARDIAN and opened his shop from 8.00 a.m. until 10.00 p.m. for all to read the current political and periodical publications. On 8 March, 1832, Heywood was arrested and appeared at the New Bailey to answer six charges in connection with selling the unstamped press. He defended himself by insisting that the POOR MAN'S GUARDIAN was not a newspaper within the meaning of the Act. He was fined £5 with £3 costs on each count, a total of £48 which he refused to pay as he considered it was unjust. He therefore served four months in the New Bailey prison. After his release, he went on to play a prominent part in the Chartist Movement and later became Mayor of Manchester.

Trade Unions

Before 1824, Trade Unions were illegal under the Combination Acts. They therefore functioned as Friendly Societies publishing their social rules but keeping their trade rules on such matters as rates of pay and hours of work, verbally. This was reflected in many titles. The FRIENDLY UNION OF MECHANICS in 1824, for example, changed its title to THE JOURNEYMEN STEAM ENGINE MAKERS' AND MILLWRIGHTS' FRIENDLY SOCIETY in 1838. In 1829 John Doherty, Secretary of the COTTON SPINNERS' UNION organised a union of all trades in the NATIONAL ASSOCIATION FOR THE PROTECTION OF LABOUR. But it was short lived.

In 1837, a MANCHESTER TRADES COUNCIL was established with R.J. Richardson from the CARPENTERS AND JOINERS as Secretary and Christopher Dean, a Stonemason as President. Edward Curren[19] was also prominent in its work. Meetings were held every Sunday and Wednesday evening at the Mosely Arms in Park Shambles. The backbone of the Council was the building trades, stonemasons, carpenters and joiners and bricklayers. Together with the textile trades, spinners, dyers, fustian cutters and hand-loom weavers, they represented about thirty trades.

Discussion in the Council ranged over political and industrial issues and action was organised arising out of their deliberations. In 1838, twenty three trades including engineering, attached their names to an Address issued by the Council. They urged all trades to boycott the procession being organised to celebrate the coronation of Queen Victoria. They condemned the political system and especially the capitalists who were riding roughshod over prostrate labour. The boycott was warmly welcomed by Manchester Universal Suffrage Association.

The stage was thus set for active participation in the Chartist rally on Kersal Moor in September, 1838.

Notes

1 KARL MARX and FREDERICK ENGELS, Collected Works.(MECW) Vol 4. Page 528.
2 MECW Vol. 4. Page 526.
3 Feargus O'Connor quoted in C.DRIVER, Life Of Oastler, Page 367.
4 MANCHESTER GUARDIAN. Quoted in J. EPSTEIN and DOROTHY THOMPSON ; The Chartist Experience. 1982. Page 127. (E and T).
5 William Cobbett (1763–1835) was a master of English and invective who championed the cause of the common people. His portrait hung in Chartist halls and premises and copies of his POLITICAL REGISTER were circulated and read among Chartists
6 Richard Oastler (1789–1861) was a vigorous campaigner on behalf of the factory children and in support of the Ten Hours Factory Act. He opposed the New Poor Law and in the late thirties increasingly called for direct action even so far as suggesting acts of sabotage. Whilst imprisoned for debt from December, 1840 to February, 1844, he issued four volumes of a periodical called FLEET PAPERS Issued From Prison.
7 MICHAEL THOMAS SADLER (1780–1835) was a pious Leeds linen merchant who in 1829 published two books condemning child labour. In the same year he was elected to Parliament where he served for the next six years and played a major part in the campaign for factory reforms.
8 SAMUEL KYDD; The History Of The Factory Movement. Vol 2 Page 42.
9 JOHN FIELDING (1784–1844) was a successful Todmorden cotton manufacturer and member of Parliament who opposed the New Poor Law and campaigned to enact the Ten Hours Bill. When it became law in 1847, it was the culmination of his political career.
10 ANTHONY ASHLEY COOPER, 7th EARL OF SHAFTSBURY (1801–1885) was born in Grosvenor Square, London. At the age of twenty five he was elected member of Parliament for Woodstock. He was a philanthropist who championed the cause of the chimney sweeps and children who worked in mines and factories.
11 Quoted in E and T Page 127

12 CHRISTOPHER DEAN (1808–?) was a stonemason and active trade unionist elected President of Manchster Trades Council in 1838. He was on the Executive Committee of the Manchester Political Union. He replaced James Wroe as Manchester delegate to the first Chartist National Convention in May, 1839. He played no part in the Movement after 1841.

13 J.W. HODGETTS was a manufacturing chemist who settled in Salford in 1831. He was elected to Salford Police Commission in 1836. Opposed New Poor law and was one of Salford Select Vestry against it in 1838. Vice President of MPU. Stood as Chartist (unsuccessful) candidate for Salford Borough in 1844.

14 ANTON DUXBURY was a provision dealer in Chapel Street, Salford and Treasurer of Salford Radical Association. Elected to Salford Select Vestry in March 1838. He opposed the New Poor Law.

15 PETER GENDALL (1799–1881) was born in Manchester and became a joiner in Islington, Salford.

16 JOSEPH RAYNOR STEPHENS (1805–1879) was a non-conformist Minister at Stalybridge who campaigned vigorously against the New Poor Law and advocated physical force to resist it. A poem written when he was imprisoned called for his freedom,
"Justice we call, to thee we bend the knee;
Redress our wrongs and set our Champion free."

17 MECW. Vol 4. Page 519.

18 HENRY HETHERINGTON (1792–1849) was publisher of THE POOR MAN'S GUARDIAN from 1831–1835. He played a prominent part in the struggle for freedom of the press against the newspaper tax dubbed by the radicals, "The Taxes on Knowledge". He wrote, "There is not another town in the country where the POOR MAN' S GUARDIAN has found so many able and warm-hearted supporters as Manchester."

19 EDWARD CURREN (1799–?) settled in Manchester from Ireland to work as a hand-loom silk weaver. He was present at Peterloo, was founding Chairman of Manchester Operative Political Union. He was active in many of the 1830s radical campaigns and became a popular Chartist full-time lecturer. He advocated repeal of the union with Ireland in addition to the Charter.

Chapter Two
Life in the City of Tall Chimneys

Coketown....was a town of red bricks, and of bricks that would have been red if the smoke and ashes had allowed it; but as matters stood it was a town of unnatural red and black like the painted face of a savage. It was a town of machinery and tall chimneys out of which interminable serpents of smoke trailed themselves for ever and ever, and never got uncoiled. It had a black canal in it, and a river that ran purple with evil-smelling dye, and vast piles of buildings full of windows where there was rattling and a trembling all day long, and where the pistons of the steam engines worked monotonously up and down like the head of an elephant in a state of melancholy madness.

Charles Dickens[1]

Manchester was described in different ways. It was the "city of tall chimneys", "the metropolis of manufacture", "a city of slums", "modern Athens", "cottonopolis" and "a capital of discontent". "Cottonopolis" obscures the diversity of its industrial base. The textile industry itself included bleaching, calico printing, glazing and dying.

In addition to textile factories, there were many large iron and brass foundries, smithies and engineering works manufacturing steam engines, machine tools, mill gearing and water wheels. Other industries included the manufacture of paper, hats, pins, rope and twine.

An observant cleric, Canon Parkinson expressed the opinion in

1841 that "There is no town in the world where the distance between rich and poor is so great or the barrier between them so difficult to be crossed."[2] Moreover, as Frederick Engels noted, the working class was "different from the middle class in speech, in thought and ideas, in culture, morals, politics and religion."[3]

Not only were there differences between the middle class and the workers, but within the working class there were wide differentials. A survey of wages in 1839 showed the die makers in calico printing earning 58 shillings for a fifty eight and a half hour week. They were the aristocrats of labour called by Feargus O'Connor, "The pompous trades and proud mechanics".[4] But at the other end of the scale, women and young men employed as piecers on self-acting mules averaged eight shillings for a sixty nine hour week. Another contemporary account calculated the average weekly income for the early 1840s of two thousand families in Ancoats, where they found that five shillings and three pence halfpenny was the norm.

There were many references to factories as "cotton bastilles", "modern hells" and "hell holes". Such descriptions were based on the extreme exploitation and cruelty with which the workers were treated, especially children who were frequently beaten and when they fell asleep, plunged into a vat of cold water. Severe punishments were meted out for lateness or misbehaviour. They included being hit with an iron rod known as the "billy roller" or hung by the hands over the machinery or even having hand-vices screwed into their ears.

A Manchester surgeon, Dr Robinson, recognised that the illness and mortality among working class children arose "from the unhealthy nature of their employment, their protracted hours of labour... the foul and contaminated conditions of the atmosphere ... and above all from their poverty and destitution."[5]

James Leach, a leading Manchester Chartist reckoned that the bitterest curse was "the hissing, whizzing, jumping, thumping, rattling, steaming and stinking factory."[6] While Thomas Carlisle expressed the horror he felt as he "heard with sound ears, the awakening of Manchester on a Monday morning at half past five by the clock: the rushing of its thousand mills, like the boom of an

Atlantic tide, ten thousand times ten thousand spools and spindles all set humming there."[7]

During periods of economic crisis and chronic unemployment, people subsisted on a meagre diet of potatoes and oatmeal with soup from a charity kitchen if they were lucky. 1841–1842 was such a period. 116 factories and 681 shops and offices were closed. Mrs Gaskell explained that for the previous three years, "trade had been getting worse and worse and the price of provisions higher and higher.... whole families went through gradual starvation in the terrible years 1839, 1840 and 1841. The indigence and suffering of the operatives induced a suspicion in the minds of many of them that their legislators, their magistrates, their employers, and even the Ministers of Religion, were in general their oppressors and enemies and were in league for their prostration and enthralment."[8]

Accidents in mills and factories were an every day occurrence. Factory cripples, men, women and children with twisted limbs and disfigured bodies were a common sight on the Manchester streets. John Doherty, leader of the Cotton Spinners who campaigned for factory reform commented, "Here is a man who, but for this system would have been of fine person and proportion. He would have stood six feet high for his arms when extended were upwards of five feet eleven inches, although he only stands five feet high. In addition to his deformity, he has lost the forefinger of his left hand from the knuckle joint and the middle finger is rendered useless by an accident at the mill."[9]

The absence of a Housing Act meant that avaricious speculators were free to erect dwellings without fear of supervision. Walls were made with only half a brick while there was only one privy and one pump to every twenty houses. There was no sanitation or drainage. The 1834 survey by Manchester Statistical Society found 10,443 houses which were "miserable abodes" for their 60,000 inhabitants. An observer noted that eight out of ten homes were the scene of misery, filth and destitution. Inspectors commented on the overcrowding. "Frequently two or more families crowded into one small house... and often more than one family lived in a damp cellar containing one room in whose pestilential atmosphere from twelve to sixteen persons were crowded."[10]

A French traveller, Alexis de Tocqueville, visited Manchester and noted that some of it was built on land "below the level of the river and overshadowed on every side by immense workshops." It was marshy ground with widely spaced ditches which could neither drain nor cleanse it. "Narrow twisting roads lead to it. They are lined with one – story houses whose ill-fitting planks and broken windows show them up, even from a distance, as the last refuge a man might find between poverty and death. Below some of these miserable dwellings is a row of cellars to which a sunken corridor leads. Twelve to fifteen human beings are crowded pell-mell into each of these damp, repulsive holes. From this foul drain the greatest stream of human industry flows out to fertilise the world. From this filthy sewer pure gold flows. Here humanity attains its most complete development and its most brutish; here civilisation makes its miracles, and civilised man is turned back almost into a savage."[11]

Few of the homes had any furniture. Bricks and logs served as chairs and tables. Bags of shavings and straw on the floor made a bed. A Pendleton poet wrote,

> The poor man's cottage stands with open door.
> See dirty pots and dishes on the floor.
> No table has he now, for them to grace.
> A three-legg'd wooden stool supplied its place;
> Seven hungry children crying round for bread,
> The father sick with kerchief round his head.[12]

Mrs Gaskell commented that the rich man cannot know what the poor man feels when he hears the piteous cry, "Daddy, a piece of bread!"[13]

Those living in the worst conditions however were not the skilled craftsmen. Their superior wages enabled them to enjoy a standard of living undreamed of by the unskilled labourers and low paid workers.

Notes

1 CHARLES DICKENS, Hard Times Chapter V
2 RICHARD PARKINSON, On The Present Condition of The Labouring Poor In Manchester, 1841.
3 MECW Vol. 4. Page 419–420. Page 124
4 NORTHERN STAR

5 Dr ROBINSON, Manchester Surgeon To The Chairman of The Select Committee On The Health of Towns, 1840. Vol. XI Appendix No. 2. Pages 221–222
6 NORTHERN STAR, 11 July, 1840.
7 THOMAS CARLISLE, Chartism, 1840. Page 82.
8 Mrs GASKELL, Mary Barton, 1906 edition. Page 67.
9 POOR MAN'S ADVOCATE, 26 May, 1832.
10 J.P. KAY, The Moral and Physical Condition of The Working Class Engaged In The Cotton Manufacture In Manchester. 1832. Page 32.
11 ALEXIS de TOCQUEVILLE, Journeys To England and Ireland, 1835. Pages 105–108.
12 MANCHESTER OBSERVER. 20 February 1819.
13 Mrs GASKELL, Mary Barton. 1906 edition. Page 44.

Chapter Three
The Kersal Moor Demonstrations

Fling out the Red Banner! o'er mountain and valley,
Let earth feel the tread of the Free once again;
Now, Soldiers of Freedom, for love of God, rally –
Old Earth yearns to know that her children are men ;

Gerald Massey[1]

The People's Charter was written as a Bill for Radical Members to present to Parliament at the same time as they presented petition forms proving how widespread dissatisfaction was among ordinary people who had no other way of expressing their discontent.

The Six Points were formulated in London and adopted in Birmingham at Newhall Hill in August, 1938. It was estimated that over two hundred thousand people had acclaimed the Charter with enthusiasm at that meeting. It had been a lively and colourful occasion with bands, processions and the election of delegates to the London Chartist Convention and it set the tone for a number of other meetings which were held around the country that Autumn.

The programme of demands were those set out in The People's Charter:

1 A vote for every man aged twenty one, of sound mind and not in prison.
2 A secret ballot.

3 No property qualifications for Members of Parliament.
4 Payment of Members
5 Equal Electoral Districts.
6 Annual Parliaments

Chartist speakers such as Feargus O'Connor and Joseph Raynor Stephens travelled far and wide passing on the message of hope that the Charter inspired. O'Connor spoke at Bolton, Sheffield, Shields, Sunderland, Keighley, Halifax and many smaller places en route. A Greater Manchester meeting was planned for Monday 24 September, 1838.

The First Kersal Moor Meeting[2]

Preparations for the meeting were thorough. Large placards were posted on the walls of every town and village for ten miles in every direction. The message informed people that at a delegate meeting on 3 September at which Mr Fletcher,[3] a surgeon from Bury was Chairman, a decision was taken to call a rally on 24th, later that month. A resolution from that preliminary meeting "respectfully requested" the owners of "manufacturies, collieries and other establishments in the neighbourhood... to close or suspend their works on the day of the meeting for the purpose of giving their workmen the opportunity of attending."

Invitations were sent to "the trades and other bodies in Manchester and the neighbouring towns and villages" to attend the demonstration which was purposely called on a Monday which, by tradition, many workmen and artisans observed as a day off. Special pleas were made to women to "recollect that on your exertions depends the success of this glorious enterprise."

Kersal Moor was a traditional meeting place where people gathered to watch races and to participate in amusements and social activity. It was well chosen as the venue for the rally. R.J. Richardson who was both Secretary of the Lancashire Anti-Poor Law Association and Manchester Political Union was one of the Marshalls. In an interview given to the Manchester Guardian reporter, he said "It is probable that every cotton mill in Manchester, and for a circuit of ten or twelve miles round, will be closed". He added that the Borough Reeve and Constables had pledged themselves to provide a posse of policemen to allay any fears of an uproar. He reported that on his return from the London meeting the previous Monday, he had stopped off in Birmingham and they had promised the attendance of their leading Chartists, Mr Atwood M.P., Mr Munz and Mr Salt[4] who would all be present and would speak. The Chair was to be taken by the well-known radical manufacturer, John Fielden who would be assisted by his brother, Thomas and Mr J.W. Hodgetts of Salford.

The Demonstration

News was circulated that thirty silk banners were in preparation and over thirty bands were booked to accompany contingents on their march to the Moor. Oldham banner was so large it had to be rigged like a mainsail with six men to carry it. Manchester banner cost fifty pounds and in addition several banners were carried which had been on the field of Peterloo when eleven people had been killed and many wounded in the charge of the military.

The authorities were so mindful of the memory of Peterloo that they postponed a review of the Horse Guards which had been scheduled to take place on the racecourse on the day of the rally. Although the owners of the racecourse protested and threatened to invoke the Trespass Act, they thought better of it in the interests of peace and order.

The Trades had been instructed to walk four abreast and at the time of Richardson's interview seventeen contingents had already been announced as participating. It was confidently expected that even the vast numbers at Peterloo would be eclipsed.

Monday 24 August dawned dull but fine. The Manchester contingent led the procession from New Cross. They went along Swan Street, Shudehill, Withy Grove, Fennel Street, Hunt's Bank and Strangeways. The Oldham contingent joined in at New Cross while those from Ashton and neighbourhood entered the town along Port Street and Ancoats Bridge.

At about half past ten a trumpeter on horseback set off along the route. He was followed by a band and a green banner inscribed UNIVERSAL SUFFRAGE, ANNUAL PARLIAMENTS, VOTE BY BALLOT and LABOUR IS THE SOURCE OF ALL WEALTH.

Another green banner read, REPEAL OF THE NEW POOR LAW with UNIVERSAL SUFFRAGE AND SHORT PARLIAMENTS on the reverse. On one banner there was a portrait of Henry Hunt,[5] the hero of Peterloo with the message, HE THAT WILL NOT WORK SHALL NOT EAT. A white banner was inscribed FOR A NATION TO BE FREE, IT IS ONLY THAT SHE WILLS IT. Could it have been carried by feminists? Possibly not because the reverse message read ENGLAND EXPECTS EVERY MAN THIS DAY TO DO HIS DUTY. The influence of the French revolution was seen in a tricolour flag inscribed THE RIGHTS OF MAN while the memory of Peterloo was invoked with a representation of the scene on St Peter's Fields and the inscription MURDER DEMANDS JUSTICE, a grim reminder that those responsible for the massacre on 16 August, 1819 had never been taken to Court.

The Trades contingents were headed by the Tailors in 105 files of five abreast. They were followed by by the Journeymen Steam Engine Makers and Millwrights Friendly Society 400 strong whose green banner carried the wordy message, EVERY MAN HAS THE RIGHT TO ONE VOTE IN THE CHOICE OF HIS REPRESENTATIVE; IT BELONGS TO HIM IN RIGHT OF HIS EXISTENCE, AND HIS PERSON IS HIS TITLE DEED. It was probably written by a committee. The 536 Associated Smiths were preceded by a banner. The Farriers, a small contingent of 39, carried a flag with UNITED TO SUPPORT, BUT NOT COMBINED TO INJURE on the front and the Farmer's Arms and GOD SAVE THE KING on the reverse.

The Metal Trades had a contingent of 64 Wheelwrights and Blacksmiths carrying a banner inscribed UNITY IS STRENGTH. They were divided from the Dyers and Dressers by a band and a white banner with PEACE AND GOODWILL TO ALL MEN on it. There were over 800 of the Dyers and Dressers and they were followed by another white banner proclaiming PRODUCTIVE CLASSES, THE FOUNDATION OF A NATION'S GREATNESS and another band.

There were a number of groups of craftsmen such as the Fustian Shearers each numbering about two hundred. The Shoemakers marched behind a banner saying SHOEMAKERS IN MANCHESTER

AND SALFORD UNITED TO MAINTAIN OUR RIGHTS INVIOLATE; PROSPERITY ATTEND OUR CAUSE. There were also the United Carpenters, the Operative Masons, the Bricklayers and the Friendly Society of Cotton Spinners who carried tricolour flags.

The Trades were followed by the political groups. Stockport Working Men's Association asserted that they were founded on the five fundamental principles of Radical Reform. The Royton Political Union with over 400 marching joined with those from Crompton who supported their local hero with the slogan DOWN WITH THE BASTILLES AND STEPHENS FOR EVER They were all well supported by bands and banners proclaiming their policies such as RELIGION WITHOUT HYPOCRISY AND POLITICS WITHOUT PARTY.

Several groups honoured leading individuals. William Cobbett and John Fielden were featured on banners. The political contingents were accompanied by fourteen cartloads of men and women, some of whom wore Caps of Liberty and carried banners referring to the foul deeds of Peterloo.

The Speakers

The speakers, John Fielden, Feargus O'Connor, Joseph Raynor Stephens were in a hackney carriage followed by the Ashton and Dukinfield contingents of over 400 people. Their banner proclaimed THE MEN OF STALYBRIDGE WILL FOLLOW FEARLESS WHEREVER FREEDOM POINTS THE WAY.

The groups who followed the route out of Manchester took thirty five minutes passing the Toll Bar leading to the Moor. There they were joined by contingents from Bury, Tottington, Unsworth, Bolton, Rochdale and Middleton who were equally colourful in presenting their case. Bury carried thirteen flags including the Union Jack, the British Ensign and others calling for UNIVERSAL SUFFRAGE, ANNUAL PARLIAMENTS, VOTE BY BALLOT and LABOUR, THE SOURCE OF ALL WEALTH. They also asserted that there should be NO TAXATION WITHOUT REPRESENTATION, harking back to the American War of Independence.

Bolton remembered Henry Hunt, the man of the people, and carried a banner inscribed with a verse:

Feargus O'Connor, showing the farms of his Land Plan

Those jealous reptiles we have not forgot,
How they did strive a patriot's name to blot;
Despite of their dungeons,
Their fines and decrees,
Who would ever bow down
To such reptiles as these?

The theme of Peterloo ran through the Northern contingents. Leigh banner was a black flag invoking the memory of THE SLAUGHTER OF OUR UNARMED AND PEACEABLE BRETHREN ON THE PLAINS OF PETERLOO, A.D. 1819. Middleton and Rochdale were less ambitious. Their smaller flag had UNITY IS STRENGTH, 1819 on one side and LIBERTY AND FRATERNITY on the other. Oldham also carried a flag surmounted by a Cap of Liberty with the message REMEMBER 16th AUGUST, 1819, PETERLOO.

As each contingent reached the Moor, bands and banners drew off to the back of the hustings while the flags were draped along the inner rail of the racecourse. Just before one o'clock when the meeting was due to start, it was estimated that there were between ten thousand and a million and a half people present. The correct number was probably in the region of 250,000.

The Platform

Among the important people on the platform were two from Salford, R.J. Richardson and R.B. Cobbett.[6] John Fielden was acclaimed as Chairman. He traced the history of assembly in large numbers back to antiquity and assured all present that they were acting in the traditional way to redress their grievances. J.W. Hodgetts also from Salford, moved a resolution calling for the People's Charter which was seconded by J.R. Stephens, the fiery orator from Stalybridge. Feargus O'Connor spoke for twenty minutes, no mean feat in the open air with such a vast audience. He said that there were over 80 acres packed with people. But in spite of the huge crowd, when he asked all those who believed that the Whigs had been guilty of treason by passing the 1832 Reform Act without including universal suffrage, a sea of hands was immediately raised.

The speakers represented the strongholds of the Movement,

Lancashire, Yorkshire, Newcastle and Birmingham. They put a number of resolutions to the meeting all of which were passed unanimously. Delegates were elected to go to London to attend the presentation of the Charter and Petition to Parliament and among them were R.J. Richardson and R.B. Cobbett.

Proceedings ended at 4.15.p.m. The bands formed up to assemble the contingents for the long walk home and the rain began to drizzle. The half dozen Police Officers who had been sent with a van and instructions not to interfere in any political matters or disputes, returned to their base in Manchester.

The People's Charter had been well launched in South Lancashire and the men, women and children who had been present, returned to their towns and villages to spread the tidings and the hope that it represented to all workers.

The 1839 Chartist Convention

During the first phase of Chartism there was an acute conflict over tactics and strategy. At the PEOPLE'S CONVENTION in February, 1839, the conflicting interests were brought into the open. Problems of tactics and organisation were discussed at length. It was clear that Parliament would not accept the petition for the Charter, but it was unclear as to what should follow. Middle class radicals had, during the campaign to achieve the 1832 Reform of Parliament, raised a revolutionary uproar and taken a threatening stance. When it came the turn of the working class to threaten insurrection, there was a fatal flaw. The slogan, PEACEFULLY IF WE CAN, FORCEFULLY IF WE MUST meant that plans for determined action were always delayed until petitions had been presented and rejected. The mass movement had, by that time, passed its peak and without a strong organisation to hold it together, entered into retreat. Those attempts at organisation and armed insurrection came to grief, particularly in Wales.

The Convention failed to solve the problem of converting a broad movement into a stable organisation. Delegates to the Convention often represented huge meetings numbering in some instances hundreds of thousands. They saw themselves as leaders with a powerful mass backing but failed to recognise that without

The National Convention as it met on 4th February 1839, at the British Coffee House.

effective and firm organisation there was no structure to hold the movement together.

The Second Kersal Moor Demonstration[7]

The second demonstration on Kersal Moor took place on 25 May, 1839. Although it was on a much smaller scale than the first, eight months earlier, it was described by R.G. Gammage, a participant and historian of the movement, as "the most formidable of all the demonstrations held about this time."[8] The establishment underestimated both the size of the demonstration and the commitment of those taking part. Estimates of the numbers vary between 30,000 and 50,000. THE TIMES reported that of the "30,000 present, the greater part seemed to be more interested in the horse races that followed the meeting than in the meeting itself."[9] The fact was that it was a holiday period and those present had chosen to be there in preference to other diversions as the Chairman, Dr Fletcher pointed out. In any case, it was unlikely that 30,000 people would arrive at 11 a.m. for a horse race that began at 2 p.m..

Two of the main speakers in a day filled with rousing orations were Dr Taylor[10] of Glasgow and Feargus O'Connor who arrived to loud cheers from the crowd. Dr Fletcher who again took the chair, arrived on horseback accompanied by a lengthy but orderly procession. By half past eleven, the rising side of the Moor was filled with spectators while the space up to the hustings was packed with thousands more. Although there were so many people present, the day passed without disturbance and the troops which had been assembled in Manchester and the surrounding districts were not needed.

The issue facing the Chartists was what form the next phase of the campaign should take. The issues of moral versus physical force had split the movement with the result that many middle class supporters were drifting away. The petition to Parliament had been rejected on 7 May when John Fielding and Thomas Attwood had requested that it be presented at the bar of the House of Commons. Their request was rejected by 235 votes to 46 and the million plus signatures were thus rendered useless. Other traditional methods of protest had also failed. With these facts in mind, the Convention proposed a number of options for discussion. Dr Fletcher, after praising his audience for "a glorious and triumphant demonstration of their zeal and energy," put the propositions to the meeting. He asked the people whether they were:

1 Prepared to withhold all money from banks or people hostile to their rights.
2 Prepared to convert money into gold.
3 Prepared to strike for a sacred month.
4 Prepared to defend the laws and constituted privileges with arms.
5 Prepared to elect Chartist candidates to stand at the next election.
6 Prepared to deal only with Chartist tradesmen.

While these propositions were considered by the crowd, a number of resolutions were put. The first, moved by Mr Walker was to the effect that peace and prosperity could only be secured by a full measure of reform based on the Charter.

Feargus O'Connor

Feargus O'Connor[11] supported the proposition and referred in his fiery contribution to the ruling by the Magistrates that the meeting was illegal and the Queen's Proclamation that it was unconstitutional. He announced to cheers that he was there as a barrister, to prove that he looked upon the meeting as both legal and constitutional and that if it was neither, the numbers present justified proceeding with it. He insisted that it was the Magistrates' caution and not the meeting that was illegal. Lord John Russell,[12] the Home Secretary had agreed that it was perfectly legal for people to meet to discuss their grievances. Amidst laughter from the crowd O'Connor said that the Queen's Proclamation was unconstitutional or alternatively that Parliament was "a set of vagabond cowards." He thought that the Queen had never possessed such grace as now when she was beset by two factions, the Whigs and the Tories. There was little difference between them he said, "If the Whigs are devils," he exclaimed, "the Tories are devils in hell"

The questions that O'Connor raised are still relevant.

> On which side are law and order? On ours? On whose side are war, strife, disorder, injustice? On the side of those who, while they

decry physical force, would govern us with the musket and the sword?

His speech was punctuated with cheers when he went on to urge them not to be bamboozled by the cry for household suffrage which he said was "a piece of humbug". He told them to look to their own franchise and assured them that, "So help me God, I am determined to have universal suffrage or I shall die in the attempt."

Supporting a resolution that called on the Government to supply the Convention with arms, Mr Rushton of Manchester expressed his regret that Henry Hunt the great orator and veteran of Peterloo was not present. He had died four years earlier, but there was still "something in his name which sent a thrill through the heart of every Radical reformer." As always, the Lancashire crowd responded to the reference to Peterloo. When Rushton said that twenty years after the event "the blood that was shed then had created a feeling which would never be extinguished until every tyrant had been swept from the face of the earth". The resolution was carried amid loud and continuous cheering. Mr Rawson of Bury who had moved the proposal said that should the request for arms be refused, they might conclude that it was the Government's intention to arm the rich against the poor and should be treated "as a declaration of war against the industrious classes."

Another rousing speech was made by Mr Aitkin[13] of Ashton. He expressed his belief in the willingness of people to assert their rights and defend their liberties. He did not wish to see the day when England would be deluged in blood, but sooner than see her sons reduced to "a state of degradation" he would lead them in the contest. The aristocracy had had their day and it was time the people had theirs. When he suggested that Lord John Russell might refuse them arms and suggested that they spare some of their hard earned money to buy them, he was greeted by cries of "We have them in thousands". He moved the resolution which called for support for the delegates to the National Convention and asked that the people defend them if they found themselves in any danger "by every means, moral and physical". Mr Hughes, an operative from Manchester seconded the resolution in a speech of considerable force in which he condemned the New Poor Law.

Monmouth Court House, during the trials of Frost, Williams, and Jones, for High Treason

At the end of the meeting, Dr Fletcher re-read the National Convention propositions which were all carried amidst loud cheering – as had been all the resolutions put during the day. The Chairman then gave thanks for the good order of proceedings and the feeling with which they had been conducted. Three cheers were given for the National Convention and The People's Charter.

The serious business over, the sports, including the horse racing which had so interested THE TIMES correspondent proceeded. Later the people returned to their homes to reflect on the resolutions that had been passed and determine how the movement should proceed.

The Way Forward

The rejection of the Petition by Parliament led to a search for a way forward. Many of the delegates saw petitioning as a waste of time and energy and favoured direct action which they called 'ulterior measures'. R.J. Richardson moved a resolution at the Chartist Convention which was in permanent session, calling for a committee to be appointed to outline a case for people to have arms. His speech was published by John Cleave[14] under the title, THE RIGHT OF ENGLISHMEN TO HAVE ARMS.

A handbill circulating in Manchester at the time asked "Dear Brothers! Now are the times to try men's souls! Are your arms ready? Have you plenty of powder and shot? Have you screwed up your courage to sticking place? Do you intend to be freemen or slaves? Are you inclined to ask for a fair day's wage for a fair day's work? Ask yourselves these questions and remember that your safety depends on the strength of your own right arm".[15]

A General Strike

William Benbow[16] had long advocated a NATIONAL HOLIDAY or SACRED MONTH. This was discussed over two days and the decision was taken to recommend a NATIONAL HOLIDAY or General Strike on 12 August. This was opposed by R.J. Richardson who had resigned from the Convention. He based his arguments on the fact that Manchester textile mills were already working short time and he regarded a call for a strike in such circumstances as foolish.

John Frost

An emergency meeting was called at the Hop Pole Inn in Hardman Street in Manchester on 6 August less than a week before the strike was due to begin. The delegates present were not in favour of the strike and the meeting was adjourned for a day or so. In the meantime, the Convention abandoned the call for a General Strike due to lack of support. In its place they decided to call for a three day NATIONAL HOLIDAY. But this decision did not receive publicity until 10 August.

Some Manchester factories closed on Monday 12 August. Others were turned out by strikers who went from one to the other appealing for support. Police and military were on the streets in some numbers and sporadic clashes occurred. On the second day, only two mills were closed and the strike therefore fizzled out.

The authorities retaliated by arresting many leaders and activists. In Wales, the arrest of Henry Vincent[17] for a defiant speech sparked an uprising. On the night of 3/4 November, five hundred armed men led by John Frost[18] marched on Newport. Fighting broke out when they reached the Westgate Hotel where soldiers were stationed. Thirty Chartists were killed or mortally wounded and more arrests followed. Between January 1839 and June 1840 nearly 500 Chartists were arrested and more than half of them imprisoned. Six Chartists including the leaders of the Newport rising were sentenced to death.

However, in spite of these draconian measures, the Chartists were not defeated. Feargus O'Connor made an appeal for action and within twenty four hours a large delegate conference assembled in Manchester on 24 February, 1840. The main business was to adopt a motion put by O'Connor to organise a demonstration throughout the country to memorialise the Queen for a Free Pardon for John Frost and Williams[19] and Jones[20] who were convicted with him.

Notes

1 THE RED REPUBLICAN, 1850 No.1
2 The account and quotations covering the 1838 demonstration are taken from THE MANCHESTER GUARDIAN, September, 1838.
3 MATTHEW FLETCHER (1795–1878) was a surgeon and veteran reformer from Bury. He had been active in the factory movement, the Reform Bill agitation and Anti-Poor Law Movement.

4 THOMAS ATTWOOD, GEORGE FREDERICK MUNZ, THOMAS CLUCKTON SALT were middle class Birmingham Radicals and leaders of the Birmingham Political Union. Attwood was a banker and Salt a lamp manufacturer.

5 HENRY HUNT (1773–1835) was a gentleman farmer in Wiltshire who achieved fame as "Orator Hunt". He was the main speaker on St Peter's Field in Manchester on 16 August, 1819. Elected member of Parliament for Preston in 1830.

6 RICHARD BAVESTOCK COBBETT (1811–1875) son of William Cobbett. He edited and published the radical journal, THE CHAMPION AND WEEKLY HERALD. He later formed a firm of solicitors in Manchester.

7 The account and quotations covering the 1839 demonstration are taken from the pamphlet, FULL REPORT OF THE GRAND MORAL DEMONSTRATION OF THE WORKING CLASSES OF SOUTH LANCASHIRE MEETING ON KERSAL MOOR, SATURDAY MAY 25TH, 1839. Published by Thomas Paine Carlile.

8 R.G. GAMMAGE, History Of The Chartist Movement. 1894 Edition. Page 113.

9 THE TIMES, 27 May, 1839.

10 JOHN TAYLOR (1805–1842) was a Naval Surgeon and also studied Theology at Glasgow. Became a radical in France. Stood in Ayr election in 1832. Edited a number of radical and Chartist journals.

11 FEARGUS O'CONNOR (1794–1855) was a barrister and brilliant orator with a sonorous voice, imposing stature, fiery red hair and gentlemanly appearance.

12 LORD JOHN RUSSELL (1792–1878) Whig Party leader and Prime Minister 1846–1852 and 1865–1866.

13 WILLIAM AITKIN was a prominent Ashton Radical and Chartist. He as a schoolmaster, poet and scientist and a leader of the 1842 General strike.

14 JOHN CLEAVE (1792–1847) was born in Ireland and became a London publisher. He edited and published several unstamped journals in the 1830s. He signed the original People's Charter and published THE ENGLISH CHARTIST CIRCULAR AND TEMPERANCE RECORD between 1841 and 1843.

15 Lt. Gen. Sir W. NAPIER KCB. Life and Opinions Of General Sir Charles James Napier GCB. Vol 2. Page 29. 1857.

16 WILLIAM BENBOW (1784–?) Manchester radical reformer from 1816. Later became a publisher in London. He toured Lancashire in the 1830s with a horse and cart selling his pamphlet GRAND NATIONAL HOLIDAY AND CONGRESS OF THE PRODUCTIVE CLASSES.

17 HENRY VINCENT (1813–1878) was a Chartist lecturer and advocate of temperance and self improvement. He travelled extensively throughout the country lecturing for the NCA.

18 JOHN FROST (1784–1877) was born in Newport and apprenticed to a bootmaker. In 1836 he was elected Mayor of Newport. He represented Newport, Carlton and Pontypool at the 1839 Chartist Convention.

Convicted of Treason in 1840, he was transported to Tasmania. He returned to Great Britain in 1856.

19 ZEPHENIA WILLIAMS (1795–1874) was a master collier and publican at Blaina. He was a free-thinker and Chartist leader. Transported to Tasmania, he became a coal owner and was joined by his wife and two children. Pardoned in 1857, he chose to remain in Tasmania.

20 WILLIAM JONES was a travelling actor from Bristol who arrived in Pontypool in 1833. He became a physical force Chartist and was deported with Frost and Williams to Tasmania.

Chapter Four
The Manchester Political Union (MPU)

Hurrah for the Charter, the good ship we sail in,
'Till the waves shall engulf us, no fears shall deform ;
But like a sea-bird, her whole voyage shall be glorious -
The Charter for ever shall weather the storm.

Edwin Gill[1]

After the Massacre of Peterloo in 1819, the Government indulged in harsh repression and the Radicals had to act with extreme caution. Small discussion groups met in houses or in a workshop. Meetings were called under the umbrella of a Benefit Society or a Botanical Club while their real purpose was only divulged to the initiated. It was a climate in which the ethos of mutual aid among reformers developed. In Manchester and Salford the Movement grew stronger. An informal economy was formed consisting of a network of co-operative stores, public houses and newsrooms as well as small traders, hawkers and vendors.

Mutuality was also reflected in collective support for victims and their families suffering from political repression. During 1840 the Manchester Relief Fund Committee paid four shillings a week to the wives of imprisoned Chartists. The Defence Fund for John Frost and the other Welsh prisoners in January 1840 was based at Abel Heywood's newsagency in Oldham Road, New Cross, R.J. Richardson's shop in Chapel Street, Salford, Thomas Barrow's drapery business[2] and T.P. Carlisle's newsagency[3] on Deansgate.

Contributions were often from a group of workers who identified themselves as SEVEN LOVERS OF JUSTICE, RED LION ROAD or A FEW SHOEMAKERS.

It was this structure that underpinned the MANCHESTER POLITICAL UNION which was re-formed in April 1838. General meetings were held on Monday evenings with discussion on Thursdays and Saturdays in Newall's Building on Market Street or the Cheese Room in Smithfield Market, New Cross. The forty one member Council met every Friday evening in Wheeler's in Whittle Street or at the Mitre Tavern in Old Church Yard.

Branches of the Union were formed in Pollard Street in November and Pendleton in December 1838. Early in 1839, Salford and Hulme and Chorlton opened in February, Whittle Street in March and Ashley Lane, Bank Top and Deansgate in June. The North East had a Branch by December and Brown Street by March, 1840.

Manchester Political Union was a loose federation. On its Executive Council were Elijah Dixon[4] from Newton, John Renner and William Willis from Salford, Philip Knight[5] from Islington, James Schofield from Ancoats, William Jackson and Robert Middleton from Hulme and Chorlton and James Redfern[6] and Thomas Davies from New Cross.

The National Charter Association (NCA)

The NATIONAL CHARTER ASSOCIATION (NCA) was formed in Manchester and Salford in July 1840 at a conference held at the Griffin Inn in Great Ancoats Street. Feargus O'Connor was the moving spirit and the local Branches of the POLITICAL UNION were the basis on which it was founded. But the local Branches guarded their autonomy jealously which created some problems for the National leadership. By law, a national organisation was prohibited from having self-governing branches. It was also illegal for autonomous organisations joined in a federation to correspond. In spite of these difficulties, Frederick Engels recognised the NCA as "the first working men's party the world ever produced."[7]

James Leach was elected President, John Campbell Secretary and Abel Heywood as Treasurer. Together with five others they formed the Executive committee to be elected each year. Each County was to have a Council with elected officers. Towns were divided into wards with classes of ten, each with a class leader. Individual members had to sign a declaration of adherence to the Charter. By April 1842, the NCA claimed 400 localities and 50,000 members. However the NCA never managed to embrace all Chartists and had problems collecting dues.

Between March 1841 and October 1842 approximately 3200 membership cards were issued in Manchester and Salford, however there were 119,280 local signatures on the 1842 Chartist petition. Formal organisation did not adequately reflect local support.

Soon after the formation of the NCA an extensive network of Branches was set up in Manchester; September 1840, Brown Street and Tib Street; October 1840, Hulme and Chorlton, Salford and Newton Heath; May 1841, Booth Street, Salford; July 1841, Salter Street; September 1841, Strand Street, Hulme; October 1841, Miles Platting; November 1841, Redfern Street; December 1841, York Street, Hulme and in April 1842, Carpenters' Hall. In many cases, however, all that had changed was the name.

Carpenters' Hall was the largest Branch with 2,000 members. In 1842 they established a library and Sunday School and by 1845 there were about 700 students in attendance. As late as 1853 there was still a functioning Library Committee with a programme of educational lectures in the arts and sciences, biography and history.

Salford Branch met in Great George Street.[8] The tradition of workers' education in Salford was well founded. From 1833 the Political Union met every Sunday evening to read and discuss radical newspapers. By 1838, Salford Working Men's Association had a reading room stocked with most of the London and provincial newspapers. Discussion classes were held every Tuesday and Friday evenings. After two years, in October, 1839 they had accumulated a library of the best political writers and asserted that "a wise people can alone be a free people."[9]

The Salford Chartists continued this tradition. In December 1840, classes were organised in Cobbett Street, at John Millington's[10] in Hope Street, at William Sumner's[11] in West Market Street, at John Campbell's in Bow Street, at Adderley Street and in

Springfield Lane. By December 1841, a year later, classes in a wide range of subjects were being organised. They included 'Capital and Labour' as understood by the Adam Smith Political Economy School. By mid 1841, Salford Chartists had also organised a library, a Sunday School and a Brass Band.

If Salford was noted for its education, other Branches were recognised for different activities. Members of the Brown Street, East Manchester Branch were known as THE MERRY CHARTISTS. They held a weekly session of dancing, singing and recitation all of which were undertaken on the purest moral principles. They had a portrait of James Wheeler in their rooms with the inscription, "That old and tried radical". When they decorated the room for a tea party in June, 1840, they added portraits of Volney,[12] Voltaire,[13] Robert Emmet,[14] George Washington,[15] William Tell[16] and Thomas Paine. Whether their wide-ranging interests stemmed from the fact that most of them were total abstainers is uncertain.

The Tib Street Branch was formed in Whittle Street but moved round the corner in 1840 as a branch of the Manchester Universal Suffrage Society. For a penny a week they had access to a subscription library and to classes for moral and intellectual improvement. After a short period they became a Branch of the National Charter Association. Many of the members were teetotal and in October 1840 they passed a resolution saying, "the practice of abstaining from intoxicating drinks has been shown.... to be founded on the best and most correct principles of moral virtue, and is well adapted to promote the progression of intelligence, and secure real happiness to man..."[17]

Many meeting places were used by both Chartist and Owenite lecturers and often they participated in joint activity. In February, 1841 the Owenite Social Missionary, Robert Buchanan[18] gave a magic lantern lecture to Tib Street NCA Branch to raise funds for the wives and families of imprisoned Chartists. Both Sunday School and Evening Classes were organised in the Branch Rooms and in 1842 the latter were held every Wednesday, Thursday and Friday to teach reading and writing.

Although Failsworth at the time was a village outside the Manchester border, to all intents and purposes it was a Manchester branch of the NCA. It had been noted for its radicalism as well as for its poets. In the 1790s a Constitutional Society was known to its opponents in the Church and King fraternity as a Jacobin Club. There were a number of sharp clashes between adherents of the two ideologies. Later the radicals were noted for their political awareness. Henry Hunt, William Cobbett and Robert Owen[19] became household names and the works of Voltaire, Thomas Paine, Robert Owen, Mirabeau[20] and Volney were found in many homes together with copies of Shakespeare and the early British poets. During the 1830s the thirst for knowledge led to the formation of both a Sunday and an Evening School.

A Branch of the NCA met in the house of Ralph Green and when that proved too small, moved to larger premises in Pew Nook. Failsworth's delegate to the NCA Council was Samuel Collins and the Branch continued to flourish until 1848.

Women's Branches

Chartist women played the part in the Movement that they always had done and still do. They were the support group raising money, organising socials, making banners and participating in whatever political activity was on the agenda. It is unclear whether they ever considered themselves as candidates for the vote at that stage. The first draft of the Charter had been in terms of universal suffrage, but that was amended to universal male suffrage on the grounds that including women might make it more difficult to obtain the vote for men.

Chartism was essentially a community campaign in which whole families took part and women were deeply involved. The majority obviously had confidence that enfranchisement of their husbands would affect the bread and butter issues which were their main concern. On the Manchester and Salford scene there are occasional glimpses of women activists which would be hidden in a national narrative. The local initiatives in terms of education, social events and processions are clear evidence of women's participation in greater strength than has been acknowledged

The question of the enfranchisement of women was certainly being discussed because R.J. Richardson wrote a pamphlet in prison in which he made the case for women playing a full part as citizens in the fullest sense, but only before they married or after they were widowed. Married women were considered to be sufficiently catered for by the responsibility which their husbands had accepted in their marriage vows. James Leach made it clear. He did not think "there was such a wide difference existed between men and women as to make it necessary for women to enjoy the suffrage. He thought that men, as fathers, husbands and brothers would secure the best interests of women".[21]

While women remained content to occupy their supporting role, the men welcomed them. But they made it clear that women should form female branches of the Manchester Political Union. It is probable that discussion at Chartist meetings was held in rooms resembling the smoke filled drinking parlours of more modern times and that the men wanted to keep them that way. In 1838, Richardson urged women to establish their own discussion groupings and Branches were formed at Pollard Street in March 1839, at Hulme and Chorlton in June, Salford in July and Brown Street in December. In December 1841 a Branch was established at Tib Street and in September of that year, a Manchester Female Victim Committee was set up. These Branches were active in raising money for the Chartist National Rent, purchasing banners, catering, making flags and taking part in parades. James Cartledge[22] made it known that he was sensitive to the position of the wives of active Chartists and said that it was "the duty of the men (of Brown Street Branch) to stop at home on Tuesday evenings in order to give their wives and sweethearts the privilege of attending the female meetings for that evening."[23]

At one such meeting held at the Chartist room, Tib Street on Wednesday 21 July, 1841, an Address was drawn up to be sent from the Female Chartists of Manchester to their Sisters of England, Ireland, Scotland and Wales. In it they said, "Our principles are justice to all, and injustice to none; a right to subsistence in the land of our birth... Sisters, if ever there was a time when it was our duty to shake off our apathy and engage in a grand struggle for liberty, surely it is now... Thousands of both males and females are walking the streets for want of employment, compelled to pledge and sell their clothes and furniture to purchase food... Our granaries are full of the food which providence has sent, and our warehouses are full of clothing, while thousands are starving ... It rests with the industrious people whether they will any longer submit to a system so wicked, fraught with injustice and misrule."[24] They asked for support in their welcome of Feargus O'Connor, James Bronterre O'Brien[25] and William Benbow who were soon to be released from prison.

They were following in a long tradition. Women were prominent on the field of Peterloo in 1819. The Failsworth contingent were led by "the beautiful and heroic Jane Winterbottom and her fair sisterhood, each clad in a vesture of white with Bay leaves woven in their hair and carrying imitation olive branches as emblems of a peaceful purpose. The black flag bearing the motto, LIBERTY OR DEATH floated behind them."[26] Women had gone to prison with Richard Carlile in the struggle for the freedom of the press and played an active part in each radical movement of the twenties and thirties. By the early 1840s they comprised nearly 60 per cent of the workforce in Manchester textile industry. Their husbands were on low wages or out of work and their main aim must have been to keep their family from destitution.

For the Kersal Moor meetings, the women organised themselves to play as significant a part as possible.They raised £50 to purchase a piece of canvas eight feet by seven and engaged a first class artist to paint a portrait of Feargus O'Connor dressed in fustian and holding a copy of the Charter in his hand. Behind him were a crowd of working people also dressed in fustian.

When the decision was taken by the NATIONAL CHARTER ASSOCIATION to engage in exclusive dealing, it was the women who boycotted or patronised shopkeepers according to their support for Chartism. William Tillman,[27] Secretary of the MANCHESTER POLITICAL UNION toured the business part of the town around Deansgate in August, 1839. He appealed for financial assistance and was successful in many cases. When he was taken before a magistrate to be prosecuted for his activity, not one shopkeeper could be found to give evidence against him.

The most articulate women in Manchester were the Owenites.

They commanded huge audiences at their lectures and among them must have been many Chartists. Frances Morrison, widow of James Morrison[28] the Editor of the Trade Union journal THE PIONEER in 1834, had edited a WOMAN'S PAGE in which she drew attention to many of the problems that beset women at that time. When her husband died, she became the resident lecturer at Salford Social Institution in Great George Street. She lectured there and at the rooms at 34 New George Street off Shudehill. At one such occasion she was described as particularly energetic in her manner, "her arguments well arranged and her remarks judiciously adapted to the occasion and characterised by remarkable simplicity and delicacy."[29] Her lecture gave rise to an animated discussion.

Emma Martin[30] became one of the best known 'infidel lecturers' who commanded audiences numbered in their thousands. She was described as "a small lady of attractive expression with dark luminous eyes, a pleasant far-reaching voice and a womanly woman."[31] At one lecture at Manchester Hall of Science on 4 September, 1844 it was reported that the room was crowded and that her talk made a very good impression.

Margaret Chapellsmith[32] was another Owenite lecturer who gave a series of four lectures at the Hall of Science to very large audiences. In their lectures these women made their demands abundantly clear. They wanted women to be given the same privileges and rights as men. They were no longer prepared to be treated as second class citizens. Twenty years later, in the sixties, their efforts bore fruit when the incipient women's suffrage campaign began to be organised although it took another fifty years of hard struggle before achieving the aim of votes for women.

Chartist Youth Sections

Both Manchester and Salford had active Youth Branches of the NCA. They held weekly joint camp meetings at Shaw's Brow on the outskirts of Salford. Salford Branch also held regular weekly meetings every Wednesday.

Brown Street Branch had a young people's section which organised Sunday evening lectures. Their Treasurer was John Hargreaves[33] whose father was a keen follower of Thomas Paine and had been active since 1831. Both father and son were elected to the NCA GENERAL COUNCIL and continued in activity through the fifties.

The Peterloo influence surfaced in the person of John Cartwright Fildes whose mother Mrs Mary Fildes[34] had been President of the Manchester Female Reformers in 1819. She was slashed across her body by one of the Yeomanry cavalry on the field, but recovered to encourage her son to play an active part in the Chartist Youth Movement throughout the 1840s.

Trade Unions and the National Charter Association

Trade Unions played a prominent and important part in the Movement for the People's Charter from the beginning. Following the debacle of the call for a Sacred Month there was a lull, but it was Chartists who dominated a meeting at Carpenters' Hall in June, 1840 called by Manchester Weavers to discuss support for the striking Stockport Power Loom Weavers. Daniel O'Donovan was in the Chair and John Campbell and Joseph Linney were among the speakers. They were all Chartists. Campbell argued that there should be a union of Power Loom Weavers both for resisting the wage reduction and for the attainment of the People's Charter.

The Chartists maintained that the political struggle was the most important and that industrial struggles were secondary. The Chartist trade unionists therefore injected a political theme into their contributions to industrial disputes. In November 1841, Manchester Trades met to discuss financial support for the London Stonemasons who were on strike. On that occasion, the Chair was occupied by James Stansfield[35] and the speakers included Benjamin Stott, Richard Littler,[36] John Bailey,[37] Alexander Hutchinson and John Murray,[38] all Chartists.

In April 1841, Peter Murray McDouall advocated the formation of industrial branches of the NCA. He visualised three types of association, those comprised of tradesmen and mechanics such as shoemakers, masons and carpenters, another of miners and agricultural workers and the third of the manufacturing workers such as spinners and weavers. He assumed that only when the members of a trades union were in support of the Charter unanimously could the group function as a Branch of the NCA. This proviso he saw as a way of ensuring that, "no police agent can be entertained at your meetings undiscovered."[39]

In November 1840, the Power Loom Weavers almost all of whom were Chartists, began to meet at the NCA Rooms at Whittle Street. They took the decision that they would support the Charter in preference to an immediate struggle to increase their wages.

A meeting of workers was held in November with 64 delegates, forty eight of whom represented 24 trades and factories. There was overwhelming support for the Charter and an amendment which aimed to add the repeal of the Corn Laws to the Chartist agenda was defeated by 59 votes to 5. James Cartledge Secretary of the South Lancashire Chartists then moved, that "all trades be recommended to join the NCA forthwith."[40]

In the following weeks and months to the end of July 1842, Manchester NCA was strengthened by the addition of the Fustian Cutters, Mechanics, Smiths, Brickmakers, Painters, Spinners, Boilermakers, Hammermen, Farriers, Shoemakers, Tailors, Carpenters and Joiners and the Power Loom Weavers.

Notes

1 THE NORTHERN STAR, 29 October, 1842

2 THOMAS BARROW was a linen draper in Deansgate. He was elected to the MPU Council in 1838/39. He was active in the Chartist Defence Fund, 1839/40 and contributed over £33 to pay fines and bail for imprisoned Chartists during the years 1839–1848.

3 THOMAS PAINE CARLILE was born in 1819 and spent part of his infancy in prison with his mother, Jane Carlile. He came to Manchester in 1836 on a speaking tour with his father. He remained and established himself as a bookseller and printer.

4 ELIJAH DIXON (1790–1876) began working in a cotton mill at eleven as a piecer and then spinner. In 1820 his health forced him to seek alternative employment and he worked as a milkman, pedlar and manufacturer of pill boxes. Active from the age of fifteen in the radical Movement, he was one of the Blanketeers who set out for London in 1817. Involved in Peterloo, he then became member of MPU in 1830. Involved in Christian Chartist Co-operative scheme to settle people on Chat Moss in 1840. Life long teetotaller and lay preacher. He was married with four children.

5 PHILLIP KNIGHT was an Overlooker in a power loom factory who lived in Islington, Manchester. a foundation member of the Hunt Memorial

Committee in 1835 and elected to the Council of MPU in October, 1838. In July 1842, he was elected to the General council of the MPU and was a strong supporter of Feargus O'Connor.

6 JAMES REDFERN was a shopkeeper in Oldham Road elected to the Council of the MPU in October, 1838. He was elected a Police Commissioner in 1838 and 1839. He was a member of the Chartist Defence Committee and Treasurer of the District Radical Electors' Association.

7 MECW Vol. 24. Page 206.

8 Great George Street had a long association with radical and working class organisations including the first Owenite Evening and Sunday School and in 1835, the first Owenite Hall of Science.

9 PAUL A. PICKERING, Chartism and Chartists In Manchester and Salford. 1995. Page 132. (Pickering)

10 JOHN MILLINGTON AND HIS WIFE SARAH were active Co-operators and Chartists. John was appointed shoemaker to the Salford Chartist Co-operative Store in 1840.

11 WILLIAM SUMNERS was a shoemaker who took over John Campbell's Newsagency after the latter was elected NCA General Secretary.

12 C.F.VOLNEY's Tract THE RUINS; OR A SURVEY OF THE REVOLUTIONS OF EMPIRES was first published in 1795 and ran through many editions. It was widely read by Radicals and Chartists.

13 FRANCOIS MARIE AROVET de VOLTAIRE was born in Paris on 21 November, 1694. He was imprisoned for a year in the Bastille after which he came to England and met English Freethinkers. His LETTERS TO THE ENGLISH was published in London in 1732.

14 ROBERT EMMET (1778–1803) was an Irish revolutionist who was executed for his part in an alleged plot to instigate an insurrection in 1802. He made a thrilling speech on the scaffold which was much admired and quoted by the Chartists.

15 GEORGE WASHINGTON (1732–1799) represented the State of Virginia at the first Constitutional Congress of the United States of America. He became the first President in May 1787.

16 WILLIAM TELL was a celebrated patriot of the Swiss resistance to Austrian invasion in 1307. The story of his being compelled to shoot an apple off his young son's head is now regarded as legend.

17 PICKERING Page 127

18 ROBERT BUCHANAN was born in Ayr in 1813. He became a school-master, Owenite missionary and journalist. He settled in Manchester and became the first full-time lecturer at the Hall of Science.

19 ROBERT OWEN (1771–1858) Inspired the working class with his vision of a Socialist Society. He was tireless in advocating his ideas about the structure of society and stimulated discussion on the evils of the Capitalist System. He is recognised as the founder of the modern Co-operative Movement and raised the demand for factory legislation by drawing attention to the terrible exploitation of children. He experimented in primary education.

20 HONORE GABRIEL RIQUETTI, COMPTE de MIRABEAU (1749–1791) became a leader of the French Revolution and President of the National Assembly. His SYSTEMS OF NATURE was published in two volumes by James Watson.

21 NEW MORAL WORLD 14 May, 1841.

22 JAMES CARTLEDGE was a factory worker who became a Methodist Preacher, Schoolmaster and Purveyor. He became a Chartist lecturer and delegate from the Brown Street Branch to South Lancashire meetings.

23 PICKERING Page 228

24 NEW MORAL WORLD 21 July 1838

25 JAMES BRONTERRE O'BRIEN (1803–1864) was described by O'Connor as "the schoolmaster of Chartism". He was educated at Trinity College, Dublin. He edited THE POOR MAN'S GUARDIAN, THE NATIONAL REFORMER and THE OPERATIVE as well as being a regular contributor to THE NORTHERN STAR.

26 BEN BRIERLEY, Failsworth My Native Village. Oldham ND Page 19.

27 WILLIAM TILLMAN (1804–?) was a ladies' shoemaker who came to Manchester from Chatham probably in the 1830s. In May 1839 he was elected Secretary of the MPU Executive Council and spoke at the second Kersal Moor demonstration. He was active in exclusive dealing for which he kept a 'black book'. Arrested in 1839, he had to be released because no shopkeeper would testify against him, but in April 1840, he was sentenced to three month's hard labour. He continued his activity on his release and in July 1840 represented Manchester at the National Delegate Conference held in Manchester. He earned £2 a week as a full time lecturer, but was removed from his job for neglecting his duty. He continued in activity however and advocated repeal of the Union with Ireland, temperance and especially female education.

28 JAMES MORRISON was a tinsmith by trade who was influenced by Owenism. Active in his Union, he played a prominent part in the struggle for the freedom of the press. He was Editor of THE PIONEER OR GRAND NATIONAL CONSOLIDATED TRADES' UNION MAGAZINE from September 1833 until it ended in July 1834.

29 FRANCES MORRISON assisted her husband in his editorial work on THE PIONEER. She took over editorship of THE LADIES PAGE which Morrison had started and changing the name to THE WOMEN's PAGE, she injected sensible down to earth feminism in trade union terms. She joined Morrison when she was fifteen and they married when she became pregnant four years or so later. They had four daughters. To help with the family finance she ran a small newspaper shop. After the death of her husband, she became a paid Owenite lecturer based in Salford at the SOCIAL INSTITUTION in Great George Street.
NEW MORAL WORLD 21 July, 1838

30 EMMA MARTIN (1812–1851) became a lecturer on educational and feminists issues after hearing an Owenite speaker in Bristol. She had an unhappy first marriage with three daughters whom she supported. She

then married Joshua Hopkins an engineering worker and had another daughter in 1847. She died at 39 from Tuberculosis. She was a courageous and hard working speaker and her publications were avidly read by women. George Jacob Holyoake in his funeral oration said she was "beautiful in expression, quick in wit, strong in will, eloquent in speech, coherent in conviction, and of stainless character. She was incomparable among public women".

31 GEORGE JACOB HOLYOAKE, History of Co-operation. 1906 Edition Page 241.

32 MARGARET CHAPPELSMITH became an advocate of freethought and an Owenite lecturer. She married John Chapellsmith and set up in business as a bookseller. Supported loyally by her husband, she lectured on such subjects as MARRIAGE IN THE NEW MORAL WORLD often being greeted by strong opposition from men but rapturous approval by women. The Chapellsmiths emigrated to America where she continued contributing articles to the local Boston paper

33 JOHN HARGREAVES was a shoemaker and member of the Oddfellows Friendly Society. He was Secretary of the Manchester Chartists in 1846.

34 Mrs MARY FILDES was President of the Manchester Female Reformers in 1819 and accompanied Henry Hunt onto the platform from which she was knocked by one of the soldiers. She called her son, Henry Hunt Fildes in honour of the hero of Peterloo.

35 JAMES STANSFIELD was a shoemaker and tailor, Chartist and Owenite. He represented both the shoemakers and tailors at delegate conferences of the Trades in 1842.

36 RICHARD LITTLER was a Salford Tailor. He was at Peterloo but came into activity in mid-1839 as a representative of Salford Radical Association on the Manchester Political Union Council. He was subsequently elected to the National Executive of the NCA. In October 1840, he became President of Salford Branch. During 1841-42 he was a Chartist lecturer and Salford representative to the South Lancashire delegate meetings. He was described as "an indefatigable friend of the people "and was involved in Salford municipal affairs. He and his wife Jane called their son Peter Feargus Littler after Feargus O'Connor whom they much admired.

37 JOHN BAILEY was a Tailor who became a shopkeeper and Chartist lecturer. He addressed public meetings during the 1842 General Strike and in September was elected Secretary of the National Chartist Defence Fund.

38 JOHN MURRAY (1777–?) was an Irish born boot and shoe maker. He was a good raconteur and claimed to have been involved with the legendary UNITED IRISHMEN in 1798 and 1803. He was a Sunday collector for the Manchester Victim Fund Committee in December 1840. He became the President of Redfern Street Branch of the NCA in 1842. He represented the Shoemakers at a meeting of Trades where he indicated that his trade would support nothing short of the Charter. Respected as a long standing Radical he was nominated by the Carpenter's Hall Branch to serve on the

NCA Council in December 1842. In 1848 he was an active member of the Manchester branch of the Irish Confederates.

39 PETER MURRAY McDOUALL'S Chartist and Republican Journal. Number 3.

40 PICKERING. Page 68.

Chapter Five
Chartist Culture

Oh! may that flame burn fierce and bright,
Within the breasts of all mankind;
May knowledge pour a flood of light
From out the intellectual mind;

Benjamin Stott[1]

In the thirties and forties of the last century, people relied on themselves for entertainment. Their zest for education was endless and they had reached a stage of class fusion where many long-held beliefs were being questioned collectively. A community based campaign such as Chartism had its own culture which was exceptionally rich. It was underpinned by the halls such as Carpenters' Hall, the Hall of Science, the People's Institute in Heyrod Street and Rev. Schofield's Chapel in Ancoats. In addition there were Chartist Rooms and premises, Temperance Hotels and Halls, radical bookshops, coffee houses, news rooms and public houses.

Talented and fluent lecturers expounded on a wide range of subjects to audiences who, for the most part were uneducated in the formal sense and in all probability could neither read nor write.They ranged through social, political and scientific topics to large numbers of people. The Chartist Schools, largely the work of women, catered for children and for the many semi-literate adults. They were held on Sundays and in the evenings as well as in informal fireside groups.

There was an extensive range of newspapers and journals for those who could read and public readings and discussion for all. The flowering of education produced considerable poetry as well as a number of novels. Frederick Engels was astonished when he arrived in Manchester towards the end of 1842 to find working men discussing the most abstruse subjects. He wrote, "I have often heard working men whose fustian jackets scarcely held together, speak upon geological, astronomical and other subjects, with more knowledge than most 'cultivated' bourgeois in Germany possess... They have translated the French Materialists, Helvetius, Holback, Diderot etc. and disseminated them, with the best English works, in cheap editions. Strauss' LIFE OF JESUS and Proudhon's PROPERTY also circulate among working men only. Shelley, the genius, the prophet, Shelley and Byron, with his glowing sensuality and his bitter satire upon our existing society, find most of their readers in the proletariat."[2]

Chartist Bookshops

There were about a dozen Chartist booksellers in Manchester and Salford and eight of the thirty local leaders were among them. They ranged from large establishments like Abel Heywood's in Oldham Street and William Willis who boasted that he had 50,000 volumes in his shop in Hanging Ditch to John Campbell in Alderley Street, Salford who was appointed Official Newsvendor to Salford Chartists. When Jacob Venedey from Leipzeig visited James Leach's bookshop in Oak Street in December, 1844 he found the publications on sale ranged from ROBIN HOOD, DICK TURPIN and ROBINSON CRUSOE to the MOVEMENT AND ANTI-PERSECUTION GAZETTE[3] and THE SPEECHES OF ROBERT EMMET ESQ. ON BEING FOUND GUILTY OF HIGH TREASON.

Robert Emmet

The Trial of Robert Emmet : a contemporary reconstruction of the scene in Green Street Courthouse

The Trial of Robert Emmet in Green Street Courthouse

The Chartists were aware that they were the heirs of a long tradition of radical struggle and paid due homage to their forebears. In particular they appreciated Robert Emmet. His portrait hung in their rooms, his story was regaled in their journals and his life and times depicted in dramatic form on the stage. In 1836 John Doherty published THE LIFE, TIMES AND CONVERSATIONS in weekly parts at a penny each. In December, 1839 Thomas Paine Carlile published Emmet's portrait in his paper, THE REGENERATOR AND ADVOCATE FOR THE UNREPRESENTED. An account of his life and trial were published in both the ENGLISH[4] and SCOTTISH CHARTIST CIRCULAR.[5]

Chartist Booksellers

THOMAS PAINE CARLILE (1819–?) had premises at 220 Deansgate. He was the son of Richard Carlile[6] and spent part of his infancy in prison with his mother, Jane Carlile.[7] He first visited Manchester in 1836 on a speaking tour and remained there as a bookseller and publisher. In 1839 he published a short-lived Journal THE REGENERATOR, AN ADVOCATE FOR THE UNREPRESENTED.

JAMES CARTLEDGE was described as a bookseller, but it is not clear whether he was a vendor or ran a bookshop. He worked in a factory, became a Methodist preacher, schoolmaster and Co-operative and Chartist lecturer. He was Secretary of Hulme and Brown Street Chartist Co-operative. He became Secretary of the South Manchester Chartist Council but resigned in 1842 to move to the Potteries.

R.J. COOPER with his brother, ROBERT,[8] was raised in a radical household. In the late 1830s he established a publishing and bookselling business in Bridge Street where he sold both the Chartist NORTHERN STAR and the Owenite NEW MORAL WORLD. He was an active Chartist, Owenite and Secularist lecturer and continued as Secretary of the Manchester Working Men's Parliamentary Association into the 1860s.

JOHN DOHERTY (1789–1854) was an Irishman, cotton spinner, trade union leader, factory reformer, printer, publisher and bookseller. Born in County Donegal, he arrived in Manchester in

1816 and became Secretary of the Cotton Spinners' Trade Union. He succeeded in uniting twenty Trade Unions in the National Association For The Protection Of Labour. In 1833 he opened Doherty's Coffee and Newsroom at 37 Withy Grove, Shudehill from 6 a.m. to 10 p.m. where 96 newspapers and periodicals were available. In 1835 the business was conducted at 4 Withy Grove as "Doherty's New Cheap Printing Office for Letterpress Printing, Copperplate and Lithographic Printing Executed With Elegance and Despatch."[9]

ABEL HEYWOOD (1810–1893) was a Chartist and Owenite bookseller, stationer and news vendor whose shop was at 56–60 Oldham Road. He belonged to the moral force Chartists. In August, 1840, he proposed the toast to the NORTHERN STAR in the Hall of Science at a celebration to welcome Peter Murray McDouall[10] and John Collins[11] on their release from prison. In 1841 he was elected Treasurer of the NCA and became a member of its Executive Committee. In 1839 he sold 40,000 newspapers, pamphlets and books each week. During 1838/39 he sold 1,800 copies of THE NORTHERN STAR[12] weekly. He was publisher and agent for a dozen periodicals ranging from the MANCHESTER AND SALFORD TEETOTAL JOURNAL to the SOCIAL PIONEER. He was also Treasurer to the Chartist National Victim Fund and collecting boxes were always prominent on his shop counter.

JAMES (1810–1869) AND HANNAH LEACH opened a bookshop in March 1842 at 110 Tib Street, but by August of that year it had moved to 40 Oak Street from where Frederick Engels bought his copies of THE NORTHERN STAR and MINERS' ADVOCATE.[13] Leach was born in Wigan and worked in a factory or in the mines until he was victimised for leading a strike. He moved to Manchester in 1826 where he became a member of the Hunt Memorial Committee in 1835. The following year he became Chairman of Manchester Radical Association and was then elected to the Council of MPU in October, 1838. He was elected Chairman at the founding conference of the National Charter Association in July, 1840. He became a lecturer and earned a reputation as a formidable orator and debater. Engels became friendly with Leach and had a good opinion of him. He described him as "known to me

John Collins

personally as an honest, trustworthy and capable man."[14] Leach's book, STUBBORN FACTS FROM THE FACTORIES was used by Engels in his own work on Manchester. After Leach was released from prison in 1848, he became a leading advocate of an alliance between the middle and working classes. Little is known about Hannah Leach or her five children, but in several instances where booksellers were active politically, the business was jointly held and was basically run by the wife.

JOSEPH (1808–1887) and MARY LINNEY. Joseph was born in Macclesfield and started work in a silk weaving mill at the age of four. He moved to Manchester in the 1830s retaining his links with the Power Loom Weavers' Union. In 1837 he played a part in an industrial dispute at Guest's Mill on the outskirts of Manchester. He became a prominent speaker and a member of the Council of the MPU. Mary was born in Blackburn. They opened a bookshop together in Garrat Road in 1839. But after Joseph's arrest and imprisonment in 1839 his health failed and they moved to Bilston in the Black Country in 1841.

REGINALD JOHN RICHARDSON (1808–1861) and ELIZABETH RICHARDSON ran a stationery, newsagent and bookseller's business at 19 Chapel Street, Salford. He was a master joiner who had to stop working at his trade after a severe accident. He then joined his wife in the business which became a centre of radical activity. He was an agent for THE NORTHERN STAR and on Saturdays his shop was said to be thronged when there were upwards of three hundred copies sold. In 1838 at the Kersal Moor demonstration he was elected Manchester delegate to the Chartist General Convention. Imprisoned in Lancaster Gaol in 1839, he wrote a pamphlet THE RIGHTS OF WOMEN.

JAMES (1791–1854) and NANCY WHEELER were printers and booksellers at 9, Whittle Street off Oldham Road. James was wounded by a sabre on St Peters Field on 16 August, 1819. At first a boot and shoe maker, he opened a bookshop in the 1830s. He was elected to the Executive Committee of the MPU and later played a leading part in establishing THE PEOPLE'S INSTITUTE in Ancoats in 1846. He was arrested for the twentieth time in 1848 but was acquitted.

WILLIAM WILLIS (1807–1861) helped Abel Heywood in the 1830s to establish his radical newsagency. Later he was employed by John Doherty and then opened his own bookshop for the sale of new and secondhand books at 5 Hanging Ditch. Due to fluctuating fortunes he moved his large stock several times. He was on the platform at the Kersal Moor demonstration in 1838 and was elected to the Council of the MPU in October of that year. He became Secretary of Salford Radical Association and agent for the Chartist Land Company.

JAMES (1798–1844) and ALICE WROE were, by 1818, established in a book and music shop at 92, Great Ancoats Street. In 1819 he became printer and publisher of THE MANCHESTER OBSERVER[15] and in August was present on the Field of Peterloo. Five weeks later he was arrested for libelling the Prince of Wales and selling illegal newspapers. He was sentenced to three years imprisonment. His wife, Alice and two brothers were subsequently also imprisoned. In 1827/28, he became part of Richard Carlile's network of supporters for the freedom of the press. In 1838 he was elected Manchester delegate to the Chartist General Convention, but resigned in May 1839, remaining an active Chartist at rank and file level. After her husband died, Alice was left in straightened circumstances with five children.

Halls and Meeting Places

CARPENTERS' HALL was at the junction of David Street (Princess Street) and Altrincham Street with a small street, Carpenters Street at the rear. It was financed by the Carpenters and joiners who raised £4500 to build it. It was large, a hundred feet long and sixty feet wide. It had a gallery seating 500 while the total capacity was about 4,000 seated. There was an orchestra gallery and an organ loft plus anti-rooms, an attic and spacious cellars. The frontage on Altrincham Street housed six or seven shops. It was used for many political and social functions as well as exhibitions and bazaars.

There was a Chartist Sunday school held in the Hall and Feargus O'Connor made a point of attending the Quarterly Examinations in 1844. In the report in THE NORTHERN STAR, it said that the hall was cheerfully thronged with parents and friends of children's education in the "democratic academy". After answering the questions put by their teachers, the children recited poems reflecting democratic aspirations such as THE DOWNFALL OF POLAND, THE FACTORY SLAVE'S LAST DAY, BYRON'S DREAM and the DEMOCRATIC WORKING MAN. O'Connor, in his address said that it was gratifying to know that there was a little army coming up who would take the field and finish the work that their fathers had so nobly begun. Leon Faucher, a French traveller also visited the hall and described the scene there, "The Carpenters' Hall is the Sunday resort of the Chartists. They open and close their meetings with the singing of democratic hymns, and their sermons are political discourses on the justice of democracy and the necessity for the Charter."[16]

THE PEOPLE'S INSTITUTE, HEYROD STREET, ANCOATS. When the Chartists lost the use of Carpenters' Hall they decided to build a new hall and were so eager to use it that they only took three months between laying the foundation stone on 10 April, 1846 and 19 July when it was officially opened. Crowds besieged the doors long before the opening time of 2 p.m., many of them groups from the country who arrived early to ensure a place. Mr Wheeler was in the Chair and a youthful Chartist, R. Sheldon Chadwick read a poem especially written for the occasion.

> Brethren and friends – thrice welcome to this Hall,
> Where friendship beckons, and where pleasures call;
> Where the bright flag of Liberty shall shed,
> Its heavenly signal o'er the patriot's head;
> Shield its defenders from the scathe of wrong,
> And guard the dome of reason and of song,
> While ye, whose hearts respond to aid our cause,
> And have the sacred splendour of our laws,
> Shall proudly see its glorious robes unfurled,
> To crush the tyrant's power and humanise the world.[17]

On another occasion, Sheldon Chadwick's brother, William Henry who was imprisoned in Kirkdale Gaol for his part in the 1848 Chartist uprising, had to be called to order by the Chairman for suggesting that, "the blow should be struck and the tyrants upset that very night."[18]

On the occasion of the opening, Feargus O'Connor was able to point out that the hall had been "erected by the zeal, the confidence and pence of working men alone".[19] At a second meeting held in the evening at 6 p.m. the veteran Radical Elijah Dixon was the speaker. He had been a Reformer all his life and was an advocate of elementary education, temperance and Co-operation. Among other speakers were Rev. James Schofield[20] from The Round House Chapel in Every Street, Ancoats and the well known radical lawyer, William Prouting Roberts[21] who had earned the title of THE MINERS' ADVOCATE. The People's Institute was not used exclusively by the Chartists. In 1852 The AMALGAMATED SOCIETY OF ENGINEERS met there to consider their position after being locked out by their employers.

THE ROUND HOUSE, EVERY STREET, ANCOATS was built by the Bible Christians for their pastor, James Schofield. He was a teetoteler, vegetarian and doctor. During the Cholera epidemic in 1833 he had won acclaim for his treatment of patients with SCHOFIELD'S CHOLERA MIXTURE. Schofield was a committed educationalist and he conducted a Sunday School and a day school at the Round House. Schofield was called the Chaplain of the Manchester Chartists. He had been on the Field of Peterloo and sharply condemned the Yeomanry Cavalry for their outrageous behaviour on that occasion. He was also one of the speakers at the Kersal Moor Chartist Rally. He was a life-long radical reformer and moral force Chartist. He was elected to the Manchester Police Commissioners from 1833–1835 and to the Town Council from 1847–1853.

Chartist Lecturers

During the early 1840s Manchester and Salford Chartists had 21 full-time paid lecturers organised on the Methodist circuit model. In Chartist rooms, chapels and halls and on outdoor meeting places, week in and week out, they drove home the Chartist message often for two hours at a stretch. Most Sundays there was a choice of four or five different lectures The subjects covered were educational and entertaining ranging from Geology to Monarchy versus Republicanism or the elative nature of the Pharisees and Saducees.

Many lecturers were, like James Leach, noted orators. Robert Gammage described him as "a man who never attempted to play the orator. In addressing a public meeting he was just as free and easy as in private conversation; but for the facts and arguments there were few of the speakers at that period who could excel him."[22] He was also reported as being "the philosopher, the philanthropist and debater; full of that statistical knowledge so highly essential to the advancement of our cause".[23]

David Ross, an Irishman taught elocution in Manchester. He was described in the press as "not only conversant with all that is pure and exalted in morality, but is a master of eloquence which melts the soul to pity and fires it with enthusiasm. His arguments are clear, powerful and effective – it is eloquence faultless."[24]

The Chartists rejected the argument that the poor had to be rescued from depravity by education. They remembered the warning given by Roland Detroiser[25] about the Manchester factory owner who looked for employees "who would work and take his glass of ale"[26] leaving him to do the thinking. Such a philosophy had never been part of radical folk lore.

Apart from the local lecturers, Manchester was a focal point for national leaders seeking an audience. Henry Vincent, the editor of THE WESTERN VINDICATOR[27] boasted that he had spoken above two hours a day for the previous thirteen months on his lecture tours.

The ever popular Feargus O'Connor was an outstanding orator. One report among many of his whistle stop tours revealed that from 18 December to 15 January he had spoken in London, Bristol, Manchester, Queenshead, Bradford, Leeds, Newcastle, Carlisle, Glasgow, Paisley and Edinburgh in the course of which he had travelled 1500 miles. However much the Chartist cause was decried in the national press, it was at meetings such as those where speakers and followers met face to face and interruptions or acclamation could convey agreement or disagreement with the outlined policy, that democratic influence could be achieved.

Chartist Sunday Schools

In 1848 plans were drawn up for a NATIONAL CHARTER ASSOCIATION SUNDAY SCHOOL UNION. This was in a situation where the majority of people were either totally illiterate or minimally educated. In addition to the Sunday Schools, lectures were advocated on political, scientific, industrial and entertaining subjects on weekday evenings. Schools should be properly conducted with instruction in reading, writing, arithmetic and general knowledge.

Frederick Engels was impressed by the education meted out in the Schools, "Here the children receive a purely proletarian education free from all the influences of the bourgeoisie; and in the reading rooms, proletarian journals, and books alone, or almost alone, are to be found."[28]

The Northern Star

Although Chartism produced a number of journals and periodicals, the only one published in Manchester was Thomas Paine Carlile's REGENERATOR, a short lived paper. However, THE NORTHERN STAR which first appeared on 18 November 1837 was eagerly read in the town and acted as a source of information and co-ordination by Manchester and Salford Chartists. At its peak the national circulation was over 36,000 but each copy was probably read aloud to ten times that number. Feargus O'Connor was the proprietor until April 1852, when George Julian Harney[29] merged it with THE FRIEND OF THE PEOPLE to become THE STAR OF FREEDOM. Its publication spanned almost the whole period of Chartist activity.

Local groups were encouraged to send in reports and it was available to be read by all in Chartist rooms and public houses. All the Chartist booksellers handled copies, some in considerable numbers. Even Ancoats Lyceum was induced to make it available in its reading room. It was a popular newspaper featuring an ARTS Page with original poetry, book reviews, extracts from British and international writing and it serialised Thomas Martin Wheeler's[30] novel, SUNSHINE AND SHADOW.

Chartist Banners and Flags

Some of the most important features of Chartist activity were public demonstrations, colourful and enjoyable occasions in which

George Julian Harney

all could participate. The banners and flags carried on them were often made collectively by men and women although some were commissioned from banner makers or artists and paid for by the hard earned pennies scraped together by groups. The making of banners was an important aspect of the development of Chartist women in particular. Working communally, they decided on the slogans and worked the designs and in so doing gained a deeper insight into the campaign. After the procession, the banners decorated the Halls and Rooms and were a constant reminder of their policy.

Chartist Poets

Poems and songs were a regular feature in the radical and Chartist journals. They were also an integral part of meetings. An audience in which there were often semi-literate individuals would be more likely to recall a message introduced in verse. In addition to the nationally well known poets such as Ernest Jones,[31] Gerald Massey[32], Thomas Cooper[33] and W.J. Linton[34] there were a number of local renown whose verse was often published anonymously.

In Manchester in the 1830s and 1840s a literary circle met at Poets' Corner at the Sun Inn in Shudehill. They published a volume called THE FESTIVE WREATH in 1842 containing a poem by Benjamin Stott. It was an elegy on John Roach, a Boilermaker and Chartist.

BENJAMIN STOTT (1813–1850) was a poet, bookbinder, trade unionist and Chartist. He was a close friend of R.J. Richardson and a life-long member of the Oddfellows Friendly Society. At the Trade Delegate Conferences during the 1842 General strike, he represented the Bookbinders. His poems, some of which were published in THE NORTHERN STAR were on subjects such as famine, liberty and the imprisoned patriot. They were published in a small volume in Middleton in 1843 as SONGS FOR THE MILLION AND OTHER POEMS. They were characteristically lucid and direct.

SAMUEL COLLINS (1802–?) was a hand loom weaver, poet, radical and Chartist who lived in Failsworth. He was an ardent supporter of William Cobbett and Henry Hunt. He was in the Failsworth contingent that walked to St Peter's Field in August, 1819. Many years later he wrote,

> In days of yore, while yet my youthful breast
> Glowed with a fierce and patriotic flame,
> Grieved for my country's sorrows unredressed,
> Regardless of the hated Sidmouth's name,
> Still pressing on allured by the beam
> Of Freedom's brightest star; the bravest, best
> The fearless Hunt's imperishable fame
> Can ne'er be shrouded in oblivion's best;
> He dared the tyrant, and exposed his crimes,
> We cheered him onward mid those dangerous times.[35]

Collins had a hard life. Ben Brierley wrote of him, "He has wrestled with poverty and experienced all the bitterness of such a struggle."[36] As a hand loom weaver with a large family, his interest in changing the system was founded on his own experience. He subscribed to THE NORTHERN STAR which was read aloud by Ben Brierley every Sunday morning during 1842 when Collins was only seventeen.

Brierley's father and Collins were "cronies in politics". He was, he said, "a genius in a way.... he never spoke at random and seemed to weigh his words."[37] Collins' poetry was published in 1859 in a slim volume. It was entitled MISCELLANEOUS POEMS AND SONGS by SAMUEL COLLINS, THE BARD OF HALE MOSS. Brierley wrote, that his poetry was "no less beautiful from appearing in uncouth garb, but if anything was more acceptable to the class of readers for whom those pages were intended."[38]

Samuel Collins had his own library of which he was very proud. He wrote a list of them on the blank end page of his copy of Thomas Paine's RIGHTS OF MAN. They showed wide ranging interests varying from Homer's ILLIAD to the COMPLETE WORKS of William Shakespeare and Volney's, RUINS OF EMPIRE as well as Paine's AGE OF REASON.

RICHARD SHELDON CHADWICK, the brother of William Henry Chadwick[39] started work at a very early age for fifteen pence a week. He attended Bennett Street Sunday School and obtained a rudimentary education. He wrote poetry which was widely acclaimed. His poem recited at the opening of the People's Institute was considered to be one of his best and most appropriate for the occasion.

He met and married the daughter of a wealthy viscount from Shropshire, but after five happy years she died leaving him with a fortune and a large London house. He then published his poems entitled POEMS OF LIFE (1854), but his wife's family milked him of his money and he retreated to live the life of a recluse in his bedroom in the house. After a short time he returned to Manchester to live in a garret.

Beer Houses and Temperance Meeting Places

In 1840 Manchester had 512 beer houses. These were not the public houses owned by large breweries but often only the front room in a house where the landlord brewed his own liquor. There were also 400 dram shops and licensed publicans. Salford had 250 beer houses and 10 spirit vaults. Some of the beer houses were used by tradesmen as houses of call where tramping artisans looking for work could call and receive a meal and a bed and be sent on their way next day if no work was available. The Braziers' Arms[40] at 42 Hodson Street, Salford was one and has retained its original appearance. Other beer houses were called after the workmen who called regularly after their day's labour. Such were The Blacksmith's Arms, 25 Downing Street, Ardwick, The Hammer In Hand in Spittal Street off Oldham Road and the Weavers' Arms in Angle Street, Chorlton on Medlock. Tradesmen doing dusty and laborious work needed to relieve their thirst and were able to report likely vacancies at their shop for the benefit of tramping artisans.

These drinking places were often the hub of working class social life offering convivial surroundings far removed from the slum dwellings where they lived. Singing, music and readings were a regular feature and most offered dominoes, a bagatelle board, drafts, cards and a good fire to sit by and indulge in discussion. Every Saturday night, "Fiddles were to be heard on all sides, and limp-looking men and pale-faced women thronged the public houses and reeled and jigged till they were turned, drunk and riotous into the streets."[41]

Among the public houses were a couple of dozen frequented by

Chartists and Trade Unionists. The National Charter Association was formed in one. John Royle who was elected to the Executive Committee of the Manchester Political Union in 1838 was landlord of the Town Hall Tavern in Chatham Street, Chorlton which was adopted as the home of the Hulme and Chorlton Chartists.

R.J. Richardson was, for a short time, a publican. Edward Nightingale was landlord of the General Abercrombie, a tap-room in Great Ancoats Street. James Leach frequented the Queen's Star in Whittle Street while the Council of the MPU met in the Mitre Inn Tavern on Hunts Bank behind the Cathedral.

However, many Chartists were total abstainers and the Temperance Movement sustained several non-alcoholic hotels and coffee shops. Most of them also sold newspapers, the MANCHESTER AND SALFORD TEMPERANCE JOURNAL and THE STAR OF TEMPERANCE. George Redfern's Temperance Hotel in George Street and Brown's Temperance Hotel in New Cross were important centres of fund-raising for the Chartist cause.

Rev. James Schofield and David Ross were both officials of local Temperance Societies. Ross argued, "There must be no domestic tyrant... no brutal father taking a slice of bread from the family to gratify an unnatural appetite for strong drink."[42] From mid 1839 all Chartist functions such as dinners, balls, festive occasions and other social functions were invariably teetotal affairs. At the 1842 Chartist Convention, Feargus O'Connor moved a resolution that delegates abstain from intoxicating drink and tobacco as an example to the movement.

Notes

1 The NORTHERN STAR, 29 October, 1842.
2 MECW Vol.4. Page 528.
3 MOVEMENT AND ANTI- PERSECUTION GAZETTE 16 November 1843 – 2 April, 1845
4 ENGLISH CHARTIST CIRCULAR AND TEMPERANCE RECORD, 1 January, 1841 – 10 January, 1844.
5 CHARTIST CIRCULAR published in Glasgow by the UNIVERSAL SUFFRAGE COMMITTEE FOR SCOTLAND between 28 September, 1839 and 9 July, 1842.
6 RICHARD CARLILE (1790–1843) was apprenticed to a tinplate worker. He moved to London from Devon and became an active radical. He

published THE REPUBLICAN and other radical and freethought journals. He was imprisoned for almost ten years for publishing seditious and blasphemous publications.

7 JANE CARLILE married Richard Carlile in 1813. They suffered an unhappy marriage and separated in 1832. There were five children, four boys and a girl. Only three of the boys survived. She became politically involved when her husband was harassed by the Government for selling radical literature. While he was in prison she kept the shop open and endured great hardship. Eventually after the Government botched one attempt to put her on trial, she was accused of seditious libel for publishing an essay by Richard in which he criticised the King for his treatment of Queen Caroline. Jane appeared without Counsel and conducted her own defence. She was sent to prison in Dorchester gaol with her husband for two years. When, in 1830, they agreed on a separation, she was given an annuity of £50 and the furniture in return for moving out of the family home. She died in 1843.

8 ROBERT COOPER (1819–1868) taught in Owenite Schools and became a lecturer and political activist. Author of many books.

9 NEW MORAL WORLD. A London Weekly Publication Developing the Principles of The Rational System of Society. 1 November, 1834 – 8 November 1845.

10 P.M. McDOUALL (1814–1853) was born in Scotland and moved to Ramsbottom at an early age. He became a doctor and enjoyed a successful practice until he threw in his lot with the Chartist cause. He became a Chartist lecturer and, after overcoming a stammer, a popular speaker with a national following. He probably emigrated to Australia and is believed to have been drowned in a shipwreck in 1853.

11 JOHN COLLINS (?–1850) was a Bible Chartist imprisoned in 1839. He was a shoemaker, a Sunday School teacher and member of the Birmingham Political Union.

12 NORTHERN STAR 5 March, 1842. "Mr James Leach, of Manchester, wishes publicly to announce that he has become Agent for the sale of the VINDICATOR, COMMONWEALTHMAN, CHARTIST CIRCULAR and all London weekly periodicals at No. 110 Tib Street, Manchester....".

13 MINERS' JOURNAL then MINERS' ADVOCATE and RECORD 21 October, 1843 – 1 May, 1845

14 MECW Vol. 4. Page 429–430.

15 MANCHESTER OBSERVER published weekly between January, 1818 and September 1832 under various titles and editors.

16 LEON FAUCHER (FAUCHER), Manchester In 1844, Its Present Condition and Future Prospect. 1844. Page 92.

17 NORTHERN STAR. 25 July, 1845.

18 T. FARMER NEWBOLD, Pages From A Life Of Strife (c1911) Pages 42 and 46.

19 NORTHERN STAR, 25 July, 1845.

20 Rev JAMES SCHOFIELD (1790–1855) was born at Colne Bridge near

Huddersfield, He was connected with the development in Lancashire of non-denominational Sunday Schools at which all-round education was provided. Both he and his son William were arrested and included in the conspiracy trial of 1842/3. All charges against William were dropped and his father was found not guilty on all counts. He died at Every Street, Ancoats on 24 April, 1855.

21 WILLIAM PROUTING ROBERTS (1806–1871) was a Chartist Barrister and legal adviser to the National Charter Association. He was Treasurer of the Chartist Co-operative Association and was Chartist candidate in the 1847 General Election in Blackburn. He was known as THE MINERS' ATTORNEY for his work in the Courts on behalf of the colliers.

22 R.G.Gammage, HISTORY OF CHARTISM, 1894 edition. Page 211.

23 NORTHERN STAR 2 April, 1842.

24 Pickering. Page 134.

25 ROLAND DETROISER (1796–1834) was apprenticed to fustian cutting. He established the first Mechanics' Institute in Hume where he gave Sunday lectures on Science and secular education. He was self-educated. He became Secretary of the National Political Union.

26 Pickering. Page 134.

27 WESTERN VINDICATOR issued weekly between 23 February and 7 December, 1839.

28 MECW Vol. 4. Page 527.

29 GEORGE JULIAN HARNEY (1817–1897) was born in London. He became a Chartist journalist and Editor of THE NORTHERN STAR. He met Frederick Engels in 1843 and became a close friend. Established THE FRATERNAL DEMOCRATS in 1844. He edited THE DEMOCRATIC REVIEW 1849–1850, THE RED REPUBLICAN 1851 and FRIEND OF THE PEOPLE 1851. He moved to America in 1867.

30 THOMAS MARTIN WHEELER (1811–1862) conducted an Owenite Social Institution and School. He was a delegate to all the Chartist conventions from 1839–1851. He delivered the main speech at the funeral of Feargus O'Connor.

31 ERNEST JONES (1819–1869) was born in Berlin where his father was an army officer. He came to England and qualified as a Barrister. He became a Chartist and was imprisoned in 1848. He led the Chartist 'left' from radicalism to socialism. After returning to the Bar in 1861 he defended a number of Fenians. He wrote poetry and prose. His funeral in Salford was the last great Chartist rally.

32 GERALD MASSEY (1828–1907) was a poet, archaeologist, Freethinker and Chartist.

33 THOMAS COOPER (1805–1892) was a self-educated man who mastered History, Greek, and Latin. He wrote poetry and novels.

34 WILLIAM JAMES LINTON (1812–1897) was a wood engraver, journalist and republican. He emigrated to America in 1848 where much of his poetry was published in journals that he edited.

35 SAMUEL COLLINS, Miscellaneous Poems. Page 35. (1859)

36 BEN BRIERLEY, Biographical Preface to Samuel Collins, Miscellaneous Poems Page XI (BP)
37 BEN BRIERLEY, Home Memories. c1882. Page 61.
38 BEN BRIERLEY, BP Page XII
39 WILLIAM HENRY CHADWICK (1829–1908) was a Chartist, Trade Unionist and Liberal propagandist. He was appointed Corresponding Secretary to the Manchester Chartists at the age of nineteen having attended Bennett Street Lancasterian School to obtain an elementary education. He later became a trade union leader for the textile workers and lecturer on Home Rule, Land Reform and Temperance.
40 THE BRAZIER'S ARMS was a House of Call for tramping Braziers where the landlord kept the Tramp Book at the bar.
41 PICKERING Page 128
42 PICKERING Page 126.

Chapter Six
Chartism and Owenism

Community doth wealth increase,
Extends the years of life,
Begins on earth the reign of peace
And ends the reign of strife.

Anon[1]

Many Chartists were also followers of Robert Owen and subscribed to his doctrines. Frederick Engels characterised the Chartists as class conscious but theoretically backward. The Owenites were more far seeing and had a better understanding of the state of the society in which they lived. In Owen's BOOK OF THE NEW MORAL WORLD they found "the most comprehensive building prospect of the future communist community".[2]

Manchester and Salford were strongholds of both Chartism and Owenism. In 1840, Robert Buchanan, one of Manchester's Social Missionaries, reported to the National Conference of the Association Of All Classes Of All Nations that there were at least ten thousand Owenites in Manchester excluding Salford. Salford had joined the Association as early as 1835 and had rapidly become one of the largest branches in the country, but their ideas of democracy differed from Owen's autocratic and patriarchal structure and they had demonstrated their intention of following their own ideas by electing a Committee of Management of twelve people rather than appoint Elders responsible to London.

Salford prospered and rapidly became one of the largest and most successful groups in the country. They had 440 members and their democratic constitution acted as a guide for other working class groups who based their structure on elected Officers and Councils.

Such rapid growth in membership made their schoolroom accommodation unsuitable and they determined to build a central meeting place. This was built in Great George Street and opened in 1835. It was the first of the Owenite Halls of Science.[3]

George Jacob Holyoake visited the Salford Social Institution and described that he found. "a pleasant structure costing £850 and capable of holding 600 persons." The cost had been met largely by Mr Joseph Smith, a master glazier and plumber. "One Sunday at noon," he said, "I entered Manchester, with no little astonishment at the extent of its mills, its buildings and its incessant streets. I found my way to the pretty little Social Institute which I knew existed in Salford, where I should meet with some friends familiar with my name, as it had been mentioned in the NEW MORAL WORLD, read there. Not long before, James Morrison had died. His widow, a pleasant little person was mistress of the tea-parties at the Salford Institute, where I spent the remainder of the day very happily, and heard the afternoon and evening lectures."[4]

Robert Cooper, one of the teachers in the Co-operative School in Salford, left a more detailed description of the Hall. "The windows were of stained glass, the floor carpeted, and the platform neat and elegant, ornamented with mottoes in gilt mouldings. Altogether it bore an aspect of comfort and respectability such as I never saw before or since in connection with an almost purely working class movement.[5]

Lloyd Jones,[6] one of the members, wrote, "As young men taking an interest in advanced thought, we were all zealous political reformers... this was also the time at which the struggle for an untaxed newspaper tax began. Many of us were active in this agitation, and in promoting sound legislation."[7]

By 1839, Manchester and Salford Owenites had outgrown the Social Institution. They decided to build a new hall at Camp Field on the site of the ancient Roman Fort in Manchester.

The Salford Hall was vacated on 17 December, 1839 and the new Hall of Science opened by Robert Owen in January, 1840. The building had been completed in a remarkably short time as the foundation stone had only been laid at the beginning of August. This was the finest Owenite Hall of Science and it could seat almost 3,000 people. It was described at the time as "An immense building in Camp Field, raised exclusively by the savings of the mechanics and artisans at a cost of £7,000 and which contains a lecture hall – the finest and most spacious in the town. It is tenanted by the disciples of Mr Owen. In addition to Sunday lectures on the doctrines of Socialism, they possess a day and Sunday School, and increase the number of their adherents by oratorios and festivals – by rural excursions, and by providing cheap and innocent recreation for the working classes... The large sums of money they raise prove that they belong to the wealthier portion of the working classes. Their audiences on Sunday evenings are generally crowded."[8]

Another description of the Hall[9] gives details of the building which fronted on Byrom Street.The general style of architecture was Italian. In subsequent years, lectures on scientific, economic and political subjects were delivered by full-time lecturers; concerts and parties were organised; while evening classes provided instruction in elementary education. By May, 1842 there were more than 250 pupils in attendance at the Sunday School which had been added in 1841. When that was extended to provide daily tuition, there were over a hundred scholars.

It was reported in THE NEW MORAL WORLD that the Manchester Hall was largely owned by individuals. They were "working men, principally foremen and mostly skilled operatives in their respective departments of the trades of this locality, such as machinists, engravers, founders, millwrights, smiths, carpenters, dyers, calico printers etc., men who having tasted the sweets of education, sobriety and strictly moral habits, are desirous of facilitating the means of imparting the like character and securing similar advantages to their brother workmen."[10]

When Frederick Engels arrived in Manchester in December, 1842, he soon found his way to the Hall of Science which was less than ten minutes walk from his office in Southgate. He described the Hall in an article in a Swiss paper. "In the larger towns they usually maintain a Hall where every Sunday they listen to speeches which are often polemical against Christianity and atheistic, but often also deal with some aspect of the workers' life; of their lecturers (preachers) Watts in Manchester seems at any rate to be an outstanding man, who has written some very talented pamphlets on the existence of God and on political economy."[11]

Engels soon started frequenting the Hall and participating in the debates and discussions that were carried on there. He wrote, "The English Socialists are far more principled than the French, which is especially due to the fact that they are engaged in open struggle against the various churches and do not want to have anything to do with religion."[12] As a young man who had freed himself from a background of extreme religious bigotry, this was an atmosphere in which he could feel very much at home. He expressed his impressions of the people he met there. "At first one cannot get over one's surprise at hearing in the Hall of Science the most ordinary workers speaking with a clear understanding on political, religious and social affairs ... I saw the Communist Hall which holds about 3,000 people, crowded every Sunday."[13]

Watts and Engels soon established friendly relations and had many arguments and discussions. Engels described Watts' organisation of the weekly meeting. He said that the audience sang social hymns accompanied by an orchestra and then Watts gave his address. He took his place on the platform without removing his hat and, after raising his hat as greeting to those present, "he takes off his overcoat and then sits down and delivers his lecture, which usually gives much occasion for laughter, for in these speeches the English intellect expresses itself in superabundant humour."[14]

Many of the Owenite Socialists were also active Chartists. Robert Cooper and his brother James were given a background in radicalism and secularism by their father. James became an Owenite Social Missionary and an active Chartist. Among other prominent Owenites were Abel Heywood, Isaac Higgenbottom[15] who was a Trustee of the Hall of Science and a keen supporter of Feargus O'Connor and Henry Stansfield.[16] But there were Chartists who were not Owenites such as Elijah Dixon. Working men who approached Chartism from the non-comformist angle, found Owen's secularism more than they could comprehend. Benjamin Stott was one whose attraction to Chartism was through his religion. He wrote,

> Our God is good, His works are fair.
> His gifts to men are real and rare.[17]

The close association of the Owenites and Chartists was evident when Manchester Owenites provided tea for Feargus O'Connor in October, 1841. About fifteen hundred Chartists, many of whom were also Owenites, sat down to tea in the Hall of Science.

However their basic differences were acknowledged and often discussed. In a lengthy article in THE NEW MORAL WORLD entitled "WILL CHARTISM BE AN EFFECTUAL REMEDY FOR NATIONAL EVILS?" the weakness of Chartism was exposed. "Will the right to vote destroy the monopoly of power?... The landlord would still have the same sway over his vassal; money would hold its power. Clerical power would not be abated... nor would knowledge of what justice awards be more. "[18]

As the call for a General Strike gathered momentum in 1842, a number of Owenites considered it their duty to go among the Chartists to beg them not to risk the cause of progress by taking action which "could only end in failure and needless bloodshed."[19] On a theoretical level, John Watts and Jonathon Bairstow debated for three nights running in October, 1843. The report in THE NEW MORAL WORLD commented "Mr Bairstow is a young man of talent, but evidently deficient in the power of reasoning. His declamation and oratory gave him a great display, but could not enforce the conviction which Mr Watts seemed to do every time he spoke". They ended by asserting that "Socialism is superior and will sooner produce the good desired by the human race."[20]

Frederick Engels attended the debate and urged the Socialists to show the Chartists that their Communes, "would not place mankind under an unbound despotism as Mr Bairstow saw in his discussion with Mr Watts". He urged them to show that real liberty and real equality would only be possible under community arrangements. He said, "Justice demands such arrangements and you will have us on your side."[21] Engels saw the strengths and weakness in both Owenism and Chartism and concluded that, "the union of Socialism with Chartism... will be the next step... Only then when this has been achieved, will the working class be the true intellectual leader of England."[22]

Notes

1 Quoted in EDMUND AND RUTH FROW, The New Moral World: Robert Owen and Owenism in Manchster and Salford. Frontispiece.
2 MECW Vol. 25. Page 253.
3 The Salford Hall of Science was in that part of Great George Street near Peru Street.
4 G.J. HOLYOAKE, Sixty Years Of An Agitator's Life. 1892. Vol. 1. Pages 71/72.
5 NATIONAL REFORMER, 14 June and 26 July, 1868.
6 LLOYD JONES (1811–1886) was born at Brandon, County Cork. He moved to Salford in 1827 and became an Owenite Social Missionary. He was also an active trade unionist, Co-operator, writer and debater.
7 LLOYD JONES, The Life, Times, and Labours of Robert Owen. 1805 ed. Page 268.
8 FAUCHER. Page 25.
9 W.R. CREDLAND, The Manchester Public Free Libraries, 1899 Manchester.
10 NEW MORAL WORLD, 4 April, 1840.
11 MECW. Vol. 3. Pages 385–389.
12 MECW. Vol. 3. Pages 385–389.
13 MECW. Vol. 3. Pages 385–389.
14 MECW. Vol. 3. Pages 385–389.
15 ISAAC HIGGENBOTTOM was an engraver and active trade unionist, Chartist and Owenite. He engraved the commemoration plate issued for the opening of Manchester Hall of Science.
16 JAMES STANSFIELD was a shoemaker and tailor. He was an active Owenite and Chartist. He represented the Shoemakers and Tailors at the Trade Conferences in 1842.
17 B. STOTT, Songs For The Million. Middleton, 1843. Pages 9/10.
18 NEW MORAL WORLD, 18 December, 1841.
19 NEW MORAL WORLD. 18 December, 1841.
20 JONOTHAN BAIRSTOW (1822–1853) was born in Leicester and became a hand-loom weaver and Chartist lecturer. He represented Bristol, Gloucester and Cheltenham at the Trade Conferences in Manchester in 1842. He left England for Australia with PETER McDOUALL and appears to have drowned off the coast of Australia in 1853.
21 NEW MORAL WORLD, 28 October, 1843.
22 MECW. Vol 3. Page 398.

Chapter Seven
The General Strike of 1842

Multitudes, that none can number,
In that season of their power,
Shall arise, as from a slumber,
Chartists wakened in an hour
Of Liberty.

Anon

When the workers at William Bailey's, Brothers Mill in Dukinfield stopped work on 4 August, 1842 they were in militant mood. Their employer was enforcing a 25% wage reduction on their already abysmally low standard of living.

On Saturday 6 August they went in procession to Hyde returning via Newton. As they approached each mill on their route the operatives ceased work and joined them. The following day, the strikers assembled on Mottram Moor, a popular place for Chartist Camp Meetings. A crowd of between four and five thousand was addressed by William Muirhouse, the Hyde Chartist Bellman.

John Leach,[1] also a Chartist from Hyde spoke of the fact that the Church had become an open hell filled by cotton lords who were a set of thieves and rogues. He called for a general strike throughout Lancashire and Cheshire which would succeed in winning the People's Charter.

These arguments made sense to the local leaders who were convinced that the only way to halt the incessant wage cuts was through a general strike of all workers. By the following Tuesday, all work in Dukinfield, Ashton and Stalybridge districts had ceased. The pattern of workers marching from mill to mill appealing for solidarity action was extremely effective. A crowd of some thousands assembled in Ashton. They proceeded along Ashton New Road with the intention of reaching Manchester to spread the strike. At the junction of Pollard Street and Great Ancoats Street they were met by the Stipendiary Magistrate, Daniel Maude and Sir Charles Shaw,[2] Chief Commissioner of Police. He was in favour of using force to stop the strikers from entering Manchester. But Maude, with Peterloo in mind, managed to restrain him.

The strikers therefore proceeded to Stevenson's Square[3] with small parties detaching themselves from the main body and going from mill to mill to gain reinforcements. In the Square, they found that the military had taken occupation and their way to the Royal Exchange was barred. So they went down Portland Street and Sackville Street onto Granby Row Fields.[4] There they obtained the use of a cart and held a meeting.

Richard Pilling,[5] an Ashton Chartist, was elected Chairman and among those who addressed the crowd were Patrick Brophy,[6] Secretary of the Irish Universal Suffrage Association, William Dixon,[7] Manchester Correspondent for the NORTHERN STAR and Christopher Doyle[8] of the Power Loom Weavers' Union. When the mills and factories closed at twelve o'clock, the crowd swelled to over twenty thousand. At half past one, the proceedings closed with three cheers for the People's Charter.

These events had an electrifying effect. The Manchester workers who were already on strike started systematically turning out other mills. By the Wednesday evening, almost all Manchester and Salford work was at a standstill. The strike started to assume a different aspect.

The Mechanics[9] convened an open air meeting of millwrights, mechanics, smiths, moulders and engineers. They met near the Gas Works on Oxford Road. A party of the Rifle Brigade charged the meeting and one man had a bayonet through his head. The Mechanics dispersed immediately but agreed to re-convene later in the day at the Sherwood Inn. There they decided to call a public

Procession of strikers, Manchester, New Cross, 1842

Procession of strikers, Manchester, New Cross, 1842

meeting of all metal trades at six o'clock the following morning at Carpenters' Hall.

On 11 August the Hall was full and among the nine resolutions passed was one calling for the strike to continue until the Peoples' Charter became the law of the land. A Committee was appointed to attempt to unite all trades behind the strike.[10]

The Manchester Power Loom Weavers who had recently joined the NCA, called a delegate meeting with a representative from each factory. Their President, Daniel Donovan[11] and Secretary, Maurice Donovan were both NCA Councillors. Mill hands and allied trades decided to organise a Trade Conference at the Fustian Cutters' Room at 70 Tib Street. The textile workers passed two resolutions. One declared that the aim of the strike was to obtain the Peoples' Charter and the other that the operatives were the guardians of law and order.

The pattern was set of the two main groups of workers, those in the metal trades and those working in the textile industry, both meeting as trade groups and each section joining together in a Trade Conference meeting at Carpenters' Hall. Leading trade unionists such as Richard Pilling, Daniel Donovan, Alexander Hutchinson[12] and Charles Stuart,[13] who were also Chartists, were thus able to play a decisive role in the strike. The solidarity and co-ordinated organisation helped to increase morale and generate enthusiasm among the strikers.

On Saturday 13th a further Trades Conference was convened with three hundred and fifty eight delegates meeting in the large room at the Sherwood Inn in Tib Street. John Middleton, a mechanic was elected as chairman. A unanimous decision was taken to post placards with the slogan:

> JUSTICE! PEACE!! LAW!!! ORDER!!!!
> The Trades of Britain carried THE REFORM BILL
> The Trades of Britain shall carry THE CHARTER[14]

Innumerable meetings were held during the following week. The Power Loom Weavers met at Carpenters' Hall, the Block Printers at the Fairfield Tavern in Fairfield Street while the Cotton Spinners and Card Room Workers assembled at Carpenters' Hall with an attendance of 3,000. In Oldham a public meeting of 18,000 met to elect delegates to attend the Manchester Trades Conferences. In

Bacup a similar meeting continued for an hour and twenty minutes after the RIOT ACT had been read ordering it to disperse.

The strike spread around the country affecting Glasgow, the Scottish and Welsh Coalfields and the industrial areas of England.

The Trades Organise

On Monday 15 August a Delegate Trades Conference was called in the Sherwood Inn, but the numbers increased to the stage where they had to re-convene at Carpenters' Hall at twelve o'clock. They elected Alexander Hutchinson as Chairman and Charles Stuart as Secretary. There were about 140 delegates present representing 85 trades.[15]

On the second day the Conference met at the Hall of Science where reports were given of full support for the demand for the Peoples' Charter with some support for wage increases. There was a protracted discussion along those lines which ended with Joseph Manory, a bricklayer from Manchester and F.A. Taylor,[16] a power loom weaver moving that the Charter be adopted and that delegates be sent to every part of the United Kingdom to advocate that all work should cease until the Charter became the law of the land. That resolution received 120 of the 140 votes present and was declared carried. At about five o'clock it was reported that the Hall had been surrounded by Magistrates, Police, Special Constables and Troops. Mr Beswick, the Chief Constable went into the Hall and was asked by the Chairman if he was a delegate. After identifying himself he informed the Conference that there was alarm in the neighbourhood because of the large numbers of people in and around the Hall and that he had forbidden large assemblies.

Alexander Hutchinson insisted that the meeting was legal, the gallery was open to the public and that press reporters were permitted to attend. Every effort had been made to conduct proceedings peacefully and in good order. Finding that he was unable to intimidate the Chairman, Mr Beswick called in the other Magistates and together they declared the meeting illegal. The delegates were given ten minutes to disperse. Business was then resumed and it was agreed that the Conference should meet the following morning at the Sherwood Inn. An Address was issued headed "LIBERTY to the Trades Of Manchester and Surrounding Districts". It continued by giving the decision of the delegates to adopt all legal means to carry into effect the Peoples' Charter and to cease labour until the Charter became the law of the land.[17]

The authorities watched these developments with some trepidation. On 15 August, Sir James Graham,[18] the Home Secretary, wrote to Major General Sir William Warre.[19] He said, "It is quite clear that these delegates are the directing body; they form the link between the trade unions and the Chartists and a blow struck at this confederacy goes to the heart of the evil and cuts off all its ramifications."[20] He sent a Metropolitan Police Magistrate to Manchester to give legal advice and to force the issue.

The correctness of Sir James Graham's analysis became apparent. As arrests were made, although the delegates continued to meet, their ranks became fewer. By Saturday, 20 August, Alexander Hutchinson, Charles Stuart and many more of local leaders were already behind prison bars.

The NCA Executive

While the Trades were organising, on the second day of the Delegate Conference, the NCA Executive met at the Round House in Every Street, Ancoats. It had been called to discuss the erection of a statue to the memory of Henry Hunt. But as it was Alexander Hutchinson who proposed the date and place of the meeting, the coincidence of the NCA and the Trades Conference being in session at the same time could be careful planning on his part.

McDouall, Leach and Campbell, all members of the NCA Executive, had been foremost in the campaign to secure unity of action between the Chartists and Trade Unionists with considerable success. McDouall moved a resolution at the Executive meeting that the strike for the Charter should be extended to cover the whole country. He was supported by Thomas Cooper who represented the turbulent potteries district where the strike was solid. Cooper argued that the spread of the strike "would and must be followed by a general outburst." The authorities would try to quell it but they had to be resisted. There was nothing left but a physical force struggle, he said and "We must get the people out to fight and they must be irresistible if they are united."[21] Cooper was opposed by William Hill[22] who moved a resolution against supporting a national strike for the Charter. His resolution only received six votes.

Feargus O'Connor did not oppose the call for a strike, but he was half-hearted. He told the Chartists "I would not have countenanced the present strike had it been suggested as a means of carrying the Charter."[23] McDouall drew up two Addresses which were adopted on the second day of their sitting. THE ADDRESS TO THE PEOPLE concluded with a call to all the Officers of the Association "to aid and assist in the peaceful extension of the Movement and to forward all monies for the use of the delegates who may be expressed over the country." He urged Chartists to "Support your leaders, Rally round our sacred cause; and leave the decision to the God of Justice and of Battle."[24]

The address was printed the same day and when James Leach posted a copy outside his shop in Oak Street, he was promptly arrested and charged with sedition and conspiracy. He was kept in a dark, damp and dirty cell for thirteen days without being allowed bail. There were thirteen prisoners in the cell which only had two beds infested with vermin. Eventually he was committed to take his trial in Liverpool. He was then granted bail of two securities of £200 each and a further £200 of his own. Although the money was handed into court, Leach was detained for a further ninety six hours before being released. Whilst on bail he was again arrested on a second charge of conspiracy. His bail was then two sureties of £200 with himself assessed at £400. When he finally appeared in Liverpool Court, the indictment against him was abandoned.

As well as arresting the leaders, the Government made every effort to intimidate the population by making a show of military force. The Third Battalion Grenadier Guards with artillery, and the First Regiment of Foot Guards with three wagons laden with ammunition were dispatched to Manchester. As the troops left their barracks to go to the station crowds assembled to watch them and the press reported that cries of "Don't go and slaughter your starving fellow countrymen" and "Remember you are brothers" were accompanied by groans. In Regent Street the crowds pressed so closely to the band which was playing along the route, that orders were given to fix bayonets.[25]

London was in a ferment. Many large meetings were held until the authorities issued a proclamation forbidding illegal assemblies. Troops and police were deployed for action. On Kennington Common it was reported that the horse patrol galloped into the crowd. "From all parts of the Common men were seen with blood streaming from their heads."[26]

During the second week of the strike the workers' attitudes hardened. Demands were formulated for the restoration of wage cuts imposed during the previous two years, an end to payment for gas light and truck shops and a ten hour day. These demands were agreed at mass meetings and local Trade Conferences with the understanding that they could only be implemented by ensuring that the Peoples' Charter became the law of the land.

Local Strike Committees enforced a system whereby employers had to apply for permission to finish work which had been caught in mid-process by the strike and where valuable materials were likely to be ruined. Application could also be made if work was urgently needed on humanitarian grounds. In some cases the applications were discussed in open mass meetings. Such discussions instilled confidence and class consciousness in workers who had hitherto regarded employers as a law unto themselves.

The employers did not accept such reduction in their authority graciously and it was with relief that they welcomed Lieutenant

Troops at Wilson's mill, 1842

General Sir Thomas Arbuthnot, K.C.[27] Colonel of the 52nd Light Infantry who arrived in Manchester on Tuesday 23 August with instructions from the Home Office to crush "the mad insurrection of the working classes."[28] He and Major General Sir William Warre, Army Commander of the Northern District accepted responsibility for the North and Midlands. Home Secretary, Sir James Graham determined that the time had come to abandon the velvet glove in favour of the mailed fist. In a letter to Queen Victoria he wrote, "The mobs are somewhat overawed by the vigour with which the troops have acted at Preston, at Blackburn and at Bolton. Several prisoners have been taken; The troops in self defence have been compelled to fire, several persons have been killed and wounded."[29]

In Manchester at a meeting on Granby Row Fields on Thursday 11 August at 6.30 p.m. when about ten thousand strikers were present, the Mayor accompanied by Magistrates arrived and declared the meeting illegal. General Warre then appeared with three troops of Dragoons each of thirty men, a Company of the 60th Rifle Brigade with two field pieces and ammunition wagons and fifty Artillerymen. With the Police and Special Constables already in attendance, the field was soon cleared.

On Monday 15 August a small army consisting of the First Dragoons, two Companies of the Grenadier Guards and a Company of the 58th Regiment were used to disperse the crowd which had gathered outside Carpenters' Hall where the Trades Delegates were meeting. Strenuous efforts at intimidation were used to subdue the strikers. Manchester Police Force was stretched to its limit and nearly four and a half thousand Special Constables were sworn in. Some of them were used to protect the works in which they were employed. The local authority "swore its trusty retainers as Special Constables (the German merchants in Manchester took part in this ceremony, and marched in an entirely superfluous manner through the City with their cigars in their mouths and thick truncheons in their hands.)"[30]

Other methods were also used to intimidate and subvert the strikers. A Proclamation from the Queen was read on 15 August. It condemned the wicked and illegal turn-outs and offered a reward of £50 to informants. The County and Borough Magistrates in

Manchester also issued a proclamation declaring all large assemblies illegal. By the end of the second week of the strike, the Home Secretary had succeeded in welding together all the military and civil forces into a machine under central control and leadership in order to crush the strike.

The strike did continue to extend to other districts, but the Chartist leadership did little to implement conference decisions, the repressive arm of the State was well oiled, more leaders were arrested and the central leadership of the strike could no longer function. The Trade Delegates went home and continued to conduct the strike through the local committees.

Manchester cotton spinners held a meeting on 21 August at which 19 mills were represented by 150 delegates. The Card Room Operatives and Dyers and Bleachers also met. Although the demand for the Peoples' Charter was still emphasised, inevitably local wage demands became the key issue. The Power Loom Overlookers held out to the last and it was 26 September before they resumed work. They had then been on strike for seven weeks with only four pence per week strike pay.

Arrests and harassment continued. During the sixth week of the strike on 13 September, Power Loom Weavers who gathered in Brown Street, Ancoats to collect their meagre strike pay were met by a strong force of Police and Special Constables. The crowd was attacked with bludgeons in a brutal manner and fifty persons were arrested.

The employers made every effort to get the workers in mines, mills and factories back to work. In many cases they did so by agreement with an increase in pay. Wage cuts were, in the main, defeated and some limited victories chalked up. Trade Union organisation was intact and strengthened.

Women Strikers

It is not surprising that women played an active and prominent part in the strike. In the textile industry they formed a large section of the workforce. Many of them were young girls. They had the experience of having formed NCA Branches and had taken part in demonstrations and all other aspects of Chartist activity. The strike offered opportunities of breaking out of the severe exploitation under which they suffered. While it was men who deliberated in conferences, women participated in the action at grass roots level

On the second day of the strike, a large crowd of women assembled at five thirty in the morning in Great Ancoats Street. They marched along Mill Street turning out the mills on their way. At Kennedy's Mill, the Management refused to close the factory. The women hurled stones at the windows and broke down the outer door and were about to rush in when Sir Charles Shaw arrived with a posse of Police.

> a scene thereupon took place which baffles all description. The Police charged the people sparing neither age nor sex, but laying about them right and left with their bludgeons and cutlasses; many were knocked down and beaten till they were unable to rise from the ground. The women responded with a volley of stones and the Police who had separated in fours and fives to use their bludgeons and cutlasses took off in all directions amidst the curses and execrations of the immense assembly. Only with the arrival of a detachment of Dragoons and another of the Rifle Brigade did the crowd disperse.[31]

On 15 September, pickets outside a small mill in the Oxford road area where work had commenced, broke windows. Most of the action was conducted by women with aprons filled with stones. At another mill on Stretford Road about thirty women weavers were throwing stones and seven of them were charged with riotous assembly[32] There were several such incidents along Stretford Road and Oxford Road where there were a number of smaller factories.

It was noteworthy that the young women among those who marched to Greg's Mill at Styal burned down the apprentice house used by the girls employed there.

Women also played a part in such organisational details as arranging the collection of strike pay and ensuring that food was distributed as fairly as possible. When the Manchester Magistrate, Mr Beswick visited Birley's Mill in Ancoats, he found a meeting outside the factory of women and girls who claimed it was their pay day.

Repression

The repression which followed the strike was unmatched in the nineteenth century. Over 1,500 strikers were arrested and brought to trial from the North West alone. The Government decided to separate the rank and file from the leadership, so Feargus O'Connor and the Chartists were charged with Conspiracy in the Court of The Queen's Bench in London,[33] while others were tried in Magistrates' Courts and over 700 before Special Commissions.

At the Salford Intermediate Sessions at the New Bailey on 29 August there were 31 Magistates on the Bench and a Grand Jury of 23 manufacturers, merchants and gentlemen. 199 prisoners were committed on charges of felony and 159 for misdemeanour. At the Liverpool Commission, five men were charged with having feloniously entered the premises of a Deansgate baker and stolen between 40 and 50 loaves of bread. The jury returned a guilty verdict and the men were sentenced to transportation for seven years. Five men who were charged with rioting and stealing five shillings were sentenced to fifteen years transportation.

By the time that O'Connor and the Chartists came to trial in March, 1843, government policy had taken a dramatic change. The trial which was not held in London, but in Lancaster, lasted eight days and was conducted in a low key by the Attorney General and the Judge. Thirty one of the defendants were found guilty but escaped being sentenced on a technicality.

The Government found itself in a dilemma. It recognised the need for fundamental changes in the relationships between workers and their employers. Some regard had to be given to working class aspirations but it had to be on terms acceptable to the capitalist state. In the 1843 trial, the law was used to persuade rather than coerce and an effort was made to assist in the creation of a position for organised labour within society. This policy came to fruition in the 1850s when the New Model Unions were formed by the aristocracy of labour, the male skilled craftsmen.

Notes

1 JOHN LEACH was a tailor. He represented Hyde factory workers jointly with George Candelet at the trades Delegate Conferences in Manchester in 1842.

2 SIR CHARLES SHAW a native of Ayr in Scotland, took charge of the newly created Manchester Police in October 1839. The Chartists condemned the introduction of a Police Force as "A damnable foreign police system."

3 Stevenson's Square was a popular open air meeting place from the time of Peterloo in 1819. It was not uncommon for three or four meetings to be

held at the same time each attracting a large crowd. It was often used as the rallying point for marches and demonstrations.

4 Granby Row Fields was a traditional meeting place on what was then the outskirts of the town. It was surrounded by factories and houses. It was an oblong shape excavated for future housing so that it formed a small valley. On the slopes many thousands of people could sit or stand one above the other and all see and hear the speakers. It covered an area of 98 by 52 yards.

5 RICHARD PILLING was a power loom weaver in Stockport and an active radical from the time of Peterloo. He was a trade unionist and one of the most influential strike leaders. Under his influence Stockport Working Mens' Association joined the NCA at its inception. When he was victimised for his activities, he moved to Ashton-under-Lyne and became a prominent Chartist. He emigrated to America towards the end of 1848.

6 PATRICK MURPHY BROPHY was a Wool Weaver who became a Chartist lecturer. In Dublin he sold 400 copies of the NORTHERN STAR each week. The Irish Universal Suffrage Association was formed in 1841 to further the six points of the Charter and the repeal of the legislative union joining England and Ireland.

7 WILLIAM DIXON was a Bolton Chartist and active mining trade unionist who moved to Manchester to become correspondent for the Northern Star and a Chartist lecturer. He was a teetotaller who later ran a temperance hotel in Great Ancoats Street.

8 CHRISTOPHER DOYLE, a Catholic, was born in Wexford in 1810. He emigrated to Manchester to work as a power loom weaver. He became an active trade unionist. During the winter of 1837/38 he and John Allison led a strike of the weavers at Guests' Mill. They were both arrested and imprisoned for mass picketing. During his imprisonment he was warned by an Inspector that he had little chance of finding work because of his known union activity. The Inspector noted that he was self-educated and had a mind of great astuteness. He also noted that he intended continuing his activity when released. A Chartist leader from 1838 to 1848, he turned to self-help in the fifties and became Birmingham Agent for the Friend In Need Assurance Society established by his friend Thomas Martin Wheeler.

9 Mechanics refers to members of the Journeymen Steam Engine Makers' and Millwrights' Friendly Society.

10 The Committee consisted of William Duffy, tailor and Irish Confederate, Bernard McCarthy, a Liverpool Chartist and James Melrose of the Journeymen Steam Engine Makers' and Millwrights' Friendly Society.

11 DANIEL DONOVAN (1817–?) was born in Cork and settled in Manchester as a power loom weaver. He became a popular Chartist lecturer. He played a leading part in both 1842 and 1848.

12 ALEXANDER HUTCHINSON was a smith who worked at Sharp Roberts and Co. Machine Tool Makers in Oxford Road.

13 CHARLES STUART was a mechanic working at Naysmiths in Patricroft. He was a member of the Journeymen Steam Engine Makers' and Millwrights' Friendly Society.

14 For the full text see M. JENKINS, The General Strike of 1842, (1990) Page 267. (JENKINS)

15 The Chartist delegates included William Bell, Fustian Cutter of Heywood; John Connor, Fustian Cutter; Daniel Donovan, Power Loom Weaver; Thomas Doyle, Painter; George Hadfield, Spinner; Alexander Hutchinson, Smith; Samuel Pemberton, Shoemaker; John Roberts, Boilermaker; William Robinson, Wiredrawer, Charles Rourke, Fustian Cutter; Bejamin Stott, Bookbinder; Thomas Whittaker, Joiner.

16 FREDERICK AUGUSTUS TAYLOR was the delegate from Royston to the Trades delegate Conference in Manchester in 1842. He was placed on trial with Feargus O'Connor at Lancaster in 1843.

17 For full text see Jenkins Page 207.

18 SIR JAMES GRAHAM (1792–1861) was a prominent Whig politician who filled several important Cabinet posts between 1830 and 1855. He was an unsympathetic character with a reputation for severity.

19 Major General SIR WILLIAM WARRE was harassed by requisitions for military aid which he was unable to supply. He advised the magistrates to negotiate with the strikers, when they were unable to enforce the law. He fell into disfavour with the Duke of Wellington and from August, 1842 his authority was greatly diminished.

20 Jenkins Page 159

21 THOMAS COOPER, The Life, Written by Himself. (1872) Page 208. (Cooper)

22 WILLIAM HILL (1806–1867) was born at Barnsley and was self-educated. He worked as a linen weaver and then as a schoolmaster. He was active in the Ten Hour and Anti-Poor Law Movements. He edited the NORTHERN STAR until July 1843 and subsequently edited other newspapers.

23 J. EPSTEIN and D. THOMPSON, The Chartist Experience. (1982) Page 296.

24 JENKINS. Page 270–272.

25 JENKINS Page 167.

26 JENKINS Page 171

27 SIR THOMAS ARBUTHNOT came from a Mayo family. He assumed command of the North West District succeeding Major General Sir Charles Napier in 1842.

28 Quoted in JENKINS Page 195.

29 JENKINS Page 193.

30 MECW. Vol. 4 Page 521–522.

31 JENKINS Page 214.

32 Among those charged with throwing stones were, Bridget Gatley, Sarah Massie, Esther Anderson, Jane Fletcher, Jane Hannahn, Diana Yates and Ann Scott. They were all weavers.

33 Of the 58 men on trial with Feargus O'Connor in 1843, fifteen were shoemakers. The shoemakers were the most radical artisans. They were members of Manchester Trades Council which was out in force on Kersal Moor in June, 1838 and they were the first trade to join the NCA in September, 1840.

Chapter Eight
The Land Plan

Where the corn-lands' pleasant tillage,
Over-waves the graceful hill,
And a wood-embosomed village,
Rises at O'Connorville.

Ernest Jones

Between 1843 and 1848, Chartism developed both progressive policies and also backward and utopian aspects. Feargus O'Connor determined to go ahead with his Land Plan the aim of which was to settle workers on four acres of land where they could be self - sufficient. Subscribers paid in to the fund and were drawn out to be re-housed by ballot. Those successful drew a sum of money from the fund to purchase stock and equipment. The main aim was to develop collective settlements where energies and resources could be pooled for the common good.

The Plan was inspired by examples ranging from the Diggers in the seventeenth century to the contemporary communes established by Robert Owen and his followers. The concept appealed particularly to the Manchester and Salford factory workers who had great confidence in O'Connor. Living in crowded insanitary conditions, working long exhausting hours for rapacious employers, the vision of an idyllic rural life met with an enthusiastic response.

In 1845, two branches of the Chartist Land Company were established. One was at John Murray's room in Carpenters' Hall and the other at John Millington's in Salford. A total of 87 branches

The almost unaltered front of Lowbands school building

The back of Lowbands school building, now the modern entrance to a private house

O'Connorville: an original cottage (left) has been incorporated into a larger building

O'Connorville: the school building altered into a private house

2819/12

REGISTERED
1 APR 1847
D.

NATIONAL LAND COMPANY.

PROVISIONALLY REGISTERED.

SHARES £1. 6s. EACH.

The object of this Company is to enable Working Men, for a trifling sum, to obtain possession of Land and Dwellings, upon such terms, that, by honourable and independent labour, they may maintain themselves and families in comfort and respectability.

BENEFITS ASSURED.

The following are the benefits which the Company guarantees to its members:

HOLDERS OF TWO SHARES—A COMFORTABLE HOUSE, TWO ACRES OF GOOD LAND, AND £15.

HOLDERS OF THREE SHARES—A HOUSE, THREE ACRES, AND £22. 10s.

HOLDERS OF FOUR SHARES—A HOUSE, FOUR ACRES, AND £30.

LEASES FOR EVER WILL BE GRANTED TO THE OCCUPANTS.

Thus ensuring to them the value of every improvement they may make upon their allotments. The Company affords great facilities to those members who have the means of purchasing their allotments. The rent will be moderate, as it will be regulated by a charge of 5 per cent. upon the capital expended.

The Company having been called into existence for the benefit of the WORKING CLASSES, the Rules enable the poorest to avail themselves of its advantages, as the Shares may be paid by instalments as low as

THREE PENCE PER WEEK.

THE RULES OF THE COMPANY (PRICE 4d.)

can be obtained of MR. WHEELER, the Secretary,

AT THE OFFICE, 83, DEAN STREET, SOHO, LONDON,

where members may be enrolled, and every information obtained;

Or of John Gathard

7563
J.S.C. REGISTRY OF
1 APR
1847

A handbill issued by the company early in 1847

LOT 4.

A CAPITAL

FREEHOLD ESTATE,

[illegible]

HERRINGSGATE FARM,

Most advantageously situate in the Parish of

RICKMERSWORTH,

HERTS.

COMPRISING A

Commodious Farm House,

With Barns, Stable, Cow House, Cart Lodge, Cattle Shed, and other Outbuildings, Yard, Garden, Orchard, and the following enclosures of excellent

Arable, Meadow, and (small part) Wood Land,

CONTAINING ALTOGETHER

103A. 1R.–30P.,

(LITTLE MORE OR LESS.)

Lying very compact, as will be seen by the Plan.

No. on Plan.	Description.	State.	Quantity. A.	R.	P.
1	Homestead, Yard, Garden, Orchard, &c.		3	0	25
2	Pike Field	Arable	10	1	13
3	Sheep House Field	Ditto	4	3	15
4	Wood	Wood	9	1	25
5	Hop Garden	Arable	11	3	34
6	Rick Yard Field	Ditto	7	3	35
7	Cherry Walk	Ditto	7	3	11
8	Little Field	Meadow	4	0	1
9	Chalk Dell Field	Arable	6	0	20
10	Long Field	Ditto	6	3	37
11	Ten Acres	Ditto	12	0	6
12	Upper Coney Burrows	Ditto	8	3	38
13	Lower Ditto and Dell	Ditto & Wood	9	2	31
			103	1	30

The Tithes have been commuted, and the Rent Charges apportioned on this Lot in lieu thereof are £17 3s. 0d. and £3. 8s. 6d. per annum.

This Lot will be sold subject to three Annuities of £20. each, (payable weekly) to three persons, independently of each other, of the respective ages of 62, 63, and 67 years; and the exclusive right of sporting over this Lot is reserved during the life of a gentleman aged 58 years

Land Tax, £2. 16s. 2d. per annum Quit Rent, £1 16s 10d per annum

5 Sale notice of Herringsgate (Heronsgate) farm, which became the O'Connorville estate

were established in the North of England. At its peak in July, 1847, subscriptions from the Manchester Branch totalled over £100 a week with the first four weeks in July bringing in £53, £44, £64 and £70. At its peak, the Land Company had 70,000 subscribers and about £100,000 in the Fund.

To give the Company legal status and enable the Directors to hold such large amounts of public money, William Prouting Roberts established premises at 59 Princess Street in Manchester and in Soho in London.

In December, 1845 the first Chartist Conference devoted to the Land Plan was held in Manchester. O'Connor tried to obtain full support for his Plan, but the Chartist leaders decided it was impracticable and a red herring. This did not deter the rank and file who continued to follow O'Connor. In March,1846, he acquired 103 acres of land at Herrongate, near Watford. He paid £2,344 for it and the estate was named O'Connorville.

Houses were built with a dairy, cowhouse, pigsty and henhouse so that settlers could cultivate the land with spade and fork. But the small tradesmen, mechanics and weavers who took over the allotments were unused to an outdoor life. They had little skill or knowledge as to how to cultivate the land. Many of them were even unable to bake bread and had to buy it locally.

One of the fortunate subscribers from Manchester was Christopher Doyle. In 1847 a group from Manchester arrived on May Day to an ecstatic welcome. Doyle was appointed Deputy Manager and, with T.M. Wheeler and Philip McGrath, a Director of the Land Company with two pounds a week salary. The spirit of the community was expressed in making newcomers feel at home. The scene on one such occasion was described in the NORTHERN STAR, "On entering the gates, the Band played THE CHARTIST LAND MARCH ... the first object that met our view, was a huge tri-coloured banner floating, high above an immense chestnut tree, bearing the inscription, O'CONNORVILLE; and secondly, Rebecca, the Chartist Cow, like the sacred cows of old, clothed in her vesture of tri-colour, rendered holy by the popular voice which is the voice of God; next the immense Dancing Booth, erected for the accommodation of our Chartist friends, attracting the attention of everyone. The remaining booths, for refreshment and amusement, were also of a very elegant character. Several ' Wandering Minstrels' attended, and earned the patronage of the visitors by singing 'THE PEOPLE'S FIRST ESTATE."[1]

In June, 1847, O'Connor bought three hundred acres at Minster Lovell in Oxfordshire in order to create Charterville. After he was elected to Parliament for Nottingham, Doyle was put in charge of the new colony. He lived in one of the cottages on the estate and within ten months a further eighty cottages had been built. Doyle spoke at a meeting in Brighton where he said that God gave the land to the whole human family. At first force and then fraud, by Act of Parliament, had made this land the possession of the few.

However, the problems besetting the Land Plan were rapidly coming to a head. At the end of 1848, a Chartist meeting was called at the Hall of Science to consider the future of the Land Company which was running into serious legal difficulties. Many of the three thousand people present were shareholders and when accusations of corruption, mismanagement and even misappropriation were voiced, disillusionment set in.

James Bronterre O'Brien had always opposed the Plan as historically backward looking. He argued that it was not possible to settle industrial workers in idyllic rural conditions when the capitalist economy was rapidly developing. He demanded that land should be nationalised for the benefit of all.

The end set in after the Court of Queen's Bench decided that the Land Company was not entitled to register as a Company. A petition to the House of Commons on 9 July, 1850 asked for the Land Company to be dissolved. Among the signatures was Christopher Doyle. O'Connor therefore introduced a petition in the House on 10 February, 1851 ending the Company. The Plan which had been the flagship of the Chartists in the 1840s failed because it was utopian in conception. Those who won a place in the scheme were insufficiently trained to benefit from their opportunity and in any case, the trend at that stage of capitalist development was away from the land, not back to it. The ruling class hated the ideas inherent in the Plan and took delight in its suppression in 1851.

Note

1 NORTHERN STAR

Chapter Nine
1848 The Year of Revolution

With heart to hand and hand in hand,
Ye'll find them all elate, –
And true as ever Spartan band!
The Men of Forty-eight.
Hurrah!
For the men of Forty-eight.

Gerald Massey

Irish people not only played a considerable part in the Radical and Chartist Movements, but their newspapers were well informed and events in England were followed closely in Ireland.

United Irishmen and United Englishmen took up arms in support of the Irish uprising in 1798. It was very much a two-way collaboration. Irish grievances and opposition to the Act of Union[1] were championed by William Cobbett and Henry Hunt. The Chartists continued this tradition.

Manchester had a large Irish community. In the 1841 census there were over 34,000 Irish in the town most of them living within the confines of Little Ireland and Irish Town[2]. A French visitor, Leon Faucher, commented, "In the midst of this immense population you could easily distinguish the Irish... often they assemble by hundreds at the corner of Oldham Street and Ancoats Street. One of them reads in a loud voice, the IRISH NEWS, the ADDRESSES of O'CONNELL or THE CIRCULARS OF THE REPEAL ASSOCIATION; and afterwards the whole is commented upon without end and with great clamour. They are so strictly organised, that in a twinkling of an eye, one or two thousand can be collected at any given spot."[3]

The Manchester Branch of the Loyal National (Irish) Repeal Association had five thousand members. It was financed by the Anti-Corn Law League[4] by an arrangement made between Richard Cobden[5] and Daniel O'Connell.[6] It was from its ranks that the notorious Irish "lambs" were recruited. They formed the Anti-Corn Law police who defended League speakers with blackthorn cudgels when they were involved in disputation with the Chartists.

The Manchester Council of the League was comprised of mill owners, manufacturers, merchants and bankers. To the Chartists they were, "the blood – sucking, grasping, grinding tyrants"[7] who advocated the repeal of the Corn Laws and cheap bread in order to lower wages Many members of the Irish Repeal Association were also members of the Operative Anti-Corn Law Association (OACLA)[8] which had a following in Manchester among those who supported O'Connell. Prominent Irish repealers such as John Finnigan,[9] John Kelly[10] and William Duffy were also members of the OACLA.

Chartists opposed O'Connell for his anti-trade unionism, anti-radicalism and his shady deals with the Government. A systematic campaign was conducted to expose the pretensions of the League.[11] Feargus O'Connor emphasised his differences with O'Connell and made a claim to represent the revolutionary traditions of the United Irishmen. Of the prominent leaders of Radicalism and Chartism at least fifteen in Manchester alone were Irish, a number of whom were active in the stormy events of both 1842 and 1848.[12]

In the 1843 re-organisation the NCA Executive Committee became predominately working class in character. O'Connor became the Treasurer to bolster the financial and legal position. Philip McGrath,[13] an East End tailor became President, T.M. Wheeler, a former baker and school teacher was Secretary. Thomas Clark,[14] a shoemaker and Christopher Doyle, a power loom weaver together with the officers, were designated "An Irish Mafia, daring and eloquent."[15] Frederick Engels described them as "Men who have nothing to lose, two thirds of them not having a shirt to their backs. They are the real proletarians and sans culottes, and, moreover, Irishmen – wild, headstrong, fanatical Gauls ... Give me two hundred thousand Irishmen and I could overthrow the entire British monarchy."[16]

In 1839 the Manchester Political Union established the Ashley Lane Branch in Irish Town, the stronghold of the O'Connell Irish Union Repealers. The leaders were Peter Power and Patrick Flynn[17] who were emigrant hand-loom weavers and followers of O'Connor rather than O'Connell. By 1848, Irish Town had become a centre of Chartism. It was graphically described by Engels as consisting of filthy cottages with damp unclean cellar dwellings harbouring numerous colonies of swine. The cottages had been built in an unplanned and haphazard manner.

Bad as the conditions in Irish Town were, the situation in Ireland was infinitely worse. The peasants were starving after several years of potato blight[18] and a popular uprising was in preparation.The aim was national liberation and the establishment of a Republic. The left-wing of the National Liberation Movement led by John Mitchell and James Laylor established an organisation called THE IRISH CONFEDERATION[19] Clubs were set up for training units of a National Guard who were to spearhead the uprising against British colonial rule.The Ashley Lane Branch played no small part in welding the Confederates and Chartists together. During the winter of 1847/48 a network of Irish Confederate Clubs was formed in Manchester which maintained links with the Chartist leaders in Great Ancoats Street.

When Feargus O'Connor became member of Parliament for Nottingham, he retained a passionate interest in Irish affairs. He denounced the Irish Coercion Bill of 1847[20] and was scathing about John O'Connell who was following in his father's footsteps by collaborating with "the base, bloody and brutal whigs" O'Connor won praise and support from the Confederates. James Leach and J.B. Trainor were invited to represent the NCA as guest speakers at the first anniversary meeting of the Confederates in Dublin in January, 1848.

In February, of that year, John Mitchell launched a new paper THE UNITED IRISHMEN[21] which took its motto from Wolfe Tones's tribute to "the men of no property."[22] Through the paper, Mitchell advised the peasants to pay no rates or rent and to resist eviction. He also advised them to arm and he published articles giving advice on the best way to conduct street warfare.

At first, Mitchell was wary of establishing close relations with the Chartists, but he soon adopted a more conciliatory attitude and advocated a Chartist Irish Confederation Alliance. He wrote, "They are our brothers and allies; we are bound to them, to their ends, as they offer to help us to ours. Their enemies and ours are one – the gold-broking, blood bartering, Government of England; and the main task for both of us is one – to pull down that Molock and trample it under our feet."[23]

Mitchell's paper created a sensation in Manchester. His appeal to the Chartists won a ready response. Manchester Chartists sold THE UNITED IRISHMAN together with THE NORTHERN STAR. Chartists and Confederates began to organise many aspects of activity jointly. Michael Dohney[24] spoke alongside Feargus O'Connor at a Chartist Camp Meeting on Oldham Edge on 19 March which was attended by people from a wide area around. O'Connor announced that it was "a sacred day and a sacred cause, and let every man swear to High Heaven never to abandon the Cause until Freedom has been obtained."[25] Resolutions were passed in favour of the Charter as well as for the Repeal of the Union.

The Alliance was formalised when William Smith O'Brien[26] attended a meeting at Manchester's recently built Free Trade Hall on St Patrick's Day in 1848. Feargus O'Connor, James Leach, J.J. Finnigan,[27] William Prouting Roberts, T.F. Meagher,[28] and Michael Dohney were also present. A joint committee of Confederates and Chartists was set up to "watch events and act as might be required."[29]

Frederick Engels commented, "We leave it to our readers to judge the importance of this alliance between the people of the two islands. British democracy will advance much more quickly when its ranks are swelled by two million brave and ardent Irish, and poverty stricken Ireland will at last have taken an important step towards its liberation."[30]

Government action against the Alliance

Alarmed by fraternisation between the Chartists and Confederates as well as the revolutionary upsurge throughout Europe, the Government introduced a Crown and Government Securities Bill in Parliament. Opposition in the House of Commons was led by Feargus O'Connor who proposed outright rejection of the Bill. He fought it clause by clause and re-introduced a motion calling for the repeal of the union with Ireland. Although the Irish in Parliament were a hundred strong, they disgraced themselves and only a dozen or so gave O'Connor any support and the Bill was rushed through its stages onto the Statute Book.

The Act contained a clause which would punish 'open and advised' speaking as a treasonable offense.[31] This Act, commonly known as the Treason/Felony Act, kept the death penalty for treason against the Crown, but provided lesser penalties of transportation of not less than seven years or imprisonment for two years. The Act received the Royal assent on 22 April, 1848, but before that, wholesale persecution had begun.

The Chartists and Repealers saw the Act as a Gagging Act and lampooned it in a verse which was circulated by the street ballad singers.

Now you must look before you speak
And mind what you are after,
'Tis death if you should say Repeal,
Or, please we want the Charter.
Sew up your mouths without delay,
The Government proposes,
And what the people wants to say
Must whistle through their noses.

Chorus
Mind what you say by night and day
And don't speak out of season
For everything, God Bless The Queen,
Is reckoned up high treason.

The Chartists and repealers say
In spite of wind and weather,
Both day and night we'll gain our right
By meeting all together
We can whisper where we cannot talk
And speak of might and reason

But they do say, good lack a day,
That everything is treason.[32]

Action was taken against O'Brien and Meagher for their speeches and Mitchell for his articles in THE UNITED IRISHMAN. When juries refused to convict O'Brien and Meagher, the case against Mitchell was withdrawn and prosecution under the new Act begun.

A demonstration was called for 10 April on Kennington Common at which the Chartist Petition was to be handed to Feargus O'Connor for presentation to the House of commons. The Government seized this opportunity to discredit the Chartists. They declared the plan to escort the Petition to Parliament to be illegal. It was therefore abandoned. All the repressive forces of the state were mobilised in an overwhelming show of force. A false statement was issued alleging that the Chartists intended to march on Parliament in defiance of the ban. When the Petition was delivered in a cab, and the meeting dispersed in an orderly fashion, the Government claimed a victory and covered the Chartists with derision. Chartism, however, was by no means defeated and both sides prepared for a future serious clash.

Manchester in 1848

By 1848, Manchester was changing from a manufacturing centre to a commercial metropolis and the focus of a wide manufacturing district. The clerks working in the huge warehouses in the centre of town provided recruits for the Special Constables who constituted about half the total of 11,000 regular Police.

When John Mitchell was sentenced to fourteen years transportation, fuel was added to the fire. Confederate Clubs held meetings to make arrangements to arm their members. Raffles were organised with pikes and guns as prizes. "At the corner of Gould Street and Rochdale Road, Michael Downey opened a shop for the sale of arms. His stock consisted of cutlasses with blades two feet long fastened into a wooden handle and pikes with a head two feet long."[33] Downey's shop caused a sensation in the neighbourhood which was in Irish Town.

The Chartists continued their revolutionary rhetoric. But in their terms, revolution was seen as an insurrection of a small, well-organised conspiracy and not as a popular uprising. At a meeting in

Stevenson's Square on 18 May, 1848, John West[34] was reported as having said that he was, "determined to speak treason in spite of the base, bloody and damnable Government." He advised his audience to obtain arms and said that he would go further than that and tell them that they should get pistols so that "they could shoot anyone who came in their way."[35]

On the following day, 19th, the Manchester Stipendiary Magistrate, Daniel Maude, wrote to the Home Office enclosing a selection of Police Reports and asking for guidance in the matter of seditious language. The Home Office replied that it was not prepared to recommend legal proceedings because Ministers were waiting for public opinion to harden and for juries to be selected who would convict.

A series of meetings in Manchester culminated in a call from the Irish Confederation for a mass demonstration in Stevenson's Square at noon on Wednesday 31 May. Placards were posted advertising the occasion, copies of which Mr Maude duly sent to the Home Office. The leaflet was headed

Address of the Repeal Delegates in Manchester Assembled

To all Irishmen and Democrats within 20 miles of Manchester

The leaflet ended with an appeal to give one day's labour to John Mitchell.[36]

The Chairman of the Repeal Delegates was George Archdeacon[37] an Irish orator who had opened proceedings at the Free Trade Hall meeting on 17 March where local Chartist leaders, Daniel Donovan and Edward Clark Cropper[38] were among the delegates. The Magistrates banned the Stevenson's Square meeting and prepared for trouble. At meetings held in Oldham, Stalybridge, Stockport and Newton on 29 May, resolutions were adopted agreeing to march to Stevenson's Square in spite of the ban.

On the day, Lieutenant General Arbothnot wrote to the Home Office enclosing letters from the Chief Constable at Pendleton and the Magistrate at Oldham which indicated that they had received reports that the proposed meeting in Manchester would be "numerously attended". Arbothnot gave an account of what actually took place. A large procession from Ashton and another from Oldham were proceeding along the road to Manchester when they were stopped at the Turnpike Gate on Oldham Road by a strong force of military and police. The demonstrators had turned out some of the mills along the route and were armed with pikes. They were formed up ten deep and carried a long black banner at the head of the procession.

W.H. Chadwick, an active participant recollected many years later that "thousands of miners"[39] were expected to come in the morning to Manchester. "When I rose in the morning I found cannon placed all about, and the military parading with drawn swords. I knew that these thousands of men were marching from Oldham, Royton and Shaw and at once ran for my life by Oldham Road and reached a place called Droylsden Lane. Here I met thousands of men marching in, armed with pikes and other implements of warfare."[40]

At the same time, another procession arrived at the other side of the Toll Bar from the Manchester direction estimated by the authorities to number between 500 and 1,000 men. They made no attempt to break through the cordon blocking their way. In Manchester paving stones were pulled up to use as weapons, but with troops supporting the police, the situation was kept under control. A large crowd assembled in front of the Union Workhouse demanding release of the inmates. Although the Police marched there in force, it was not until seven o'clock in the evening that they were able to disperse the crowd.

Mills continued to work during the day, but when they closed at six, the crowds were considerably supplemented. The Police Station in Oldham Road was attacked with stathes. Stalls in Smithfield Market were broken up. Arbuthnot called out two Troops of the 11th Hussars and two Companies of the 63rd Regiment to support the Police "who would have been overwhelmed if any riot had taken place."[41]

The huge show of force managed to avert a serious clash between the Authorities and the Chartists. Only a few arrests were made and by ten o'clock that night, the streets were clear.

Manchester was not on its own. Clashes took place in Bradford,

Liverpool and industrial towns in Lancashire and Yorkshire as well as in London.

On 5 June, George White[42] addressed a meeting in Manchester. A spy reported that he exhorted the audience to "follow the example of forming Clubs and Sections."[43] Clubs had a leader who drilled and instructed them while anything from Headquarters went to the Captains who then called the Sections together. He advised each of them to procure arms saying that he had both a pike and a gun. He then described in somewhat optimistic terms what had happened in Bradford on 29 May. He asserted that they had obtained control over the town and that if other towns had been equally well prepared, the outcome would have been different.

The following day, Ernest Jones addressed an evening meeting in Manchester. There, he was arrested on a charge arising from a speech he had made in Bonner's Fields in London on the previous Sunday. Subsequently Jones and five prominent London Chartists were each sentenced to two years in prison.[44] The Movement in Manchester continued with a further meeting in Stevenson's Square on Whit Monday 12 June. This was timed to coincide with meetings throughout the country. Arbuthnot expressed concern that "the clerks and others like them who had been sworn in as Special Constables were likely to leave Manchester during Whit Week to proceed to places in the country to amuse themselves in the usual way."[45] He need not have worried because the day passed without any serious clashes between the Authorities and the Chartists.

Strenuous efforts were made to penetrate the Clubs with spies. But this proved difficult as many met in private houses and excluded all but known members. In both Liverpool and Manchester, "there are few men who will run the risk of giving information, and fewer still on whom dependence could be placed." So commented the Head Constable of Liverpool who also asserted that those from whom he had obtained information "at present live in a constant state of alarm fearing that the least discovery would consign them to death."[46]

From early in the year there had been frequent meetings between Irish Repeal leaders and their followers in Manchester.

One of the main items discussed at such meetings was the need to support an insurrection in Ireland by preventing troops leaving England to re-inforce those already in occupation. This was regarded as a major problem because troops were frequently moved back and forth between the two countries during 1848.[47]

On 22 July a new journal, THE ENGLISH PATRIOT AND THE IRISH REPEALER[48] was published. It was edited by James Leach assisted by George Archdeacon and George White.

August was the critical month. During the second week, delegates assembled in Whittaker's Temperance Hotel in Great Ancoats Street and discussed plans for co-ordinated action on 15th and 16th of the month.

On the evening of 14th, seventy armed Chartists from the Working Men's Hall in Oldham made their way to Manchester where the Clubs were reported as ready for action. Hundreds waited, pike in hand for the signal to be given. In Ashton a policemen was shot which gave the Authorities the excuse to act swiftly. Three hundred armed Police, two Companies of the 30th Foot and two Troops of the Royal Irish Dragoons were deployed and on Tuesday evening 15 August, the arrests began. James Leach, Daniel Donovan, George White and George Webber[49] were arrested and taken to prison where they were shackled with handcuffs and heavy leg irons. This action and the imprisonment of the National leadership virtually destroyed the Movement.

Of the Executive Committee of five which had been elected in May, Ernest Jones and Peter Murray McDouall were imprisoned for two years each and James Leach for nine months. Feargus O'Connor was completely absorbed in his Land Plan and in any case, was not in sympathy with militant action. The other two members, Samuel Kydd[50] and John McCrea[51] lacked the national status to be effective leaders.

There was a similar situation locally. Of the twenty Commissioners elected by the National Assembly, fourteen were arrested and imprisoned. A rapid decline in morale set in and spies and informers had a field day. At the Liverpool Assizes in December, 1848, forty six Chartists and Confederates were charged with Seditious Conspiracy and Unlawful Assembly by urging people to arm and calling on them to campaign for the People's Charter and Repeal of the Act of Union with Ireland.

James Abraham Ball, a spy[52] and one of the principal witnesses for the Prosecution, alleged that the Chartists had, "taken an empty shop adjoining the Gas Works... There was to be a boring underground ... Then they were to get five hundredweight of gunpowder underneath this boring and set it on fire in order to blow up the Gas Works and put the town in complete darkness."[53] His evidence under cross examination was so contradictory, however, that the Attorney General was forced to repudiate him. He was hissed in Court and finally so discredited that the Judge ordered him to leave. But the attitude of the Judiciary towards the Chartist was made abundantly clear by the Presiding Judge, Baron Alderson who said, "These offences begin with the distress which enables people to operate upon the minds of the large number of people who are in distress... All of you must abide a severe sentence."[54] In spite of his words, in fact the sentences, compared with those issued out for lesser offences such as stealing a loaf of bread, were in some cases lenient. West, Clark Cropper, Grocott,[55] Donovan and White were each given one year in prison. Thomas Rankin[56] and William Chadwick who was only eighteen years old, received six months. In addition, they each had to supply securities amounting to £125 to ensure that at the expiration of their sentence they would keep the peace for a further two years. If they defaulted, they would be detained until the security was paid. George Julian Harney commented, "Place Fustian in the dock, let Silk Gown charge the culprit with being a physical force Chartist and insinuate that he is not exactly free from the taint of Communism and forthwith Broadcloth in the Jury box will bellow out 'GUILTY'."[57]

They were placed in a cell together in Kirkdale Prison where conditions left much to be desired. On the first day, they agreed that they would share equally and that all gifts either of food or money should go into a common stock, each man faring alike, for better or worse.[58] This operated smoothly for a few weeks until one man received a box of food and kept it for himself. However, Leach, West and White continued and maintained a close comradeship in

Ernest Jones

difficult conditions, not only sharing but also managing to collaborate in writing a series of pamphlets which were smuggled out and printed by Joseph Barker of Wortley as TRACTS FOR THE TIME, price 1d. The eight pamphlets[59] appeared between March and July, 1849 and set out a comprehensive radical manifesto. They maintained that achieving the Charter was the first step but asserted that the next step would be a transformation of society.

On their release, many Chartists were placed in the position of being unable to participate any further in the Movement. Some emigrated, others became active in the Co-operative and Trade Union Movements. Chartism continued in the 1850s with a different emphasis and under the courageous leadership of Ernest Jones.

Notes

1 Ireland had its own Parliament from 1295 to 1800. Following the defeat of the United Irishmen in 1798, the Established Church and the Presbyterian Church who both controlled pocket and rotten boroughs, were promised generous compensation if they supported union with England. In 1800 the ACT FOR THE UNION OF GREAT BRITAIN AND IRELAND was carried by 158 votes to 115 in the Irish Parliament. It then passed through the House of Commons and received the Royal Assent on 1 August, 1800

2 Irish Town was a new town built up a clay hill beyond the old town of Manchester. It was located between the Irk and St George's Road.

3 FAUCHER Page 28.

4 The Anti-Corn Law League was formed as The Anti-Corn Law Association in 1837. It changed its name in January, 1839.

5 RICHARD COBDEN (1804–1865) was a barrister, political organiser and Member of Parliament for Stalybridge elected in 1841.

6 DANIEL O'CONNELL (1775–1847) was a poor boy who made something of himself. He approved of the United Irishmen in 1798 but disapproved of their call for reform and Catholic emancipation. He became a successful lawyer and established himself as the champion of the Catholics calling for a repeal of THE ACT OF UNION. He became M.P. for Clare in 1830 and in the reformed House of Commons in 1832, represented Dublin City. In his old age he preferred Federalism to Repeal. This weakened the Movement.

7 PICKERING. Page 88.

8 The Operative Anti-Corn Law Association (OACLA) was formed to recruit workers for the League. It was not successful.

9 JOHN JOSEPH FINNIGAN was an immigrant weaver and full time lecturer for the League in the 1840s. He opposed the factory system and

the People's Charter. In 1848 he played a part in the Irish Confederate / Chartist alliance.

10 JOHN KELLY was a printer and one of O'Connel's assistants. He became Secretary of the OACLA in 1842.

11 Frederick Engels who attended a number of meetings where the Chartists and Anti-Corn Law League speakers clashed, said, "The League cannot call a single public meeting without being most ignominiously trounced by the Chartists." (MECW Vol.3 Page 383)

12 They included Daniel and Maurice Donovan, Christopher Doyle, James Leach, Thomas Clark, Patrick Brophy and John Murray.

13 PHILIP McGRATH was an East End tailor who became President of The National Charter Association. He was also a Director of O'Connor's Land Company. In the 1847 General Election he stood for Derby and polled 220 votes. As an internationalist in outlook, he joined the Fraternal Democrats and when the 1848 revolution broke out in France, was elected with Ernest Jones and George Julian Harney to address the French Provisional Government whose aim was to forge links with revolutionary and progressive movements throughout Europe.

14 THOMAS CLARK (1821–1857) was a self-confident, class conscious agitator full of zest and energy. He played a prominent part in the Chartist Movement between 1839 and 1851. His family settled in Stockport where he was Secretary of the local branch of the NCA. By 1843, he was Chartist lecturer for Cheshire. In 1843, he was elected to the Executive Committee of the NCA and in 1845 a Director of the Chartist Co-operative Land Society. In the 1847 General Election he stood as Chartist candidate for Sheffield. He died suddenly in 1857 leaving a wife and five children in poverty.

15 H.WEISSER, British Working Class Movements and Europe, 1815–1848. (1975) Page 166.

16 MECW Vol. 3. Page 389.

17 PETER POWER and PATRICK FLYNN were Irish hand-loom weavers eking out a precarious existence in Old Oak Street, off Ashley Lane in Irish Town.

18 Irish history has ben punctuated with famines and fevers. The worst was the failure of the potato crop due to blight during 1845–1849. One third of the population relied on potatoes for their main diet. While the famine was at its worst, over a million pounds worth of food was exported under armed guard. The population was reduced during the famine years from over eight million in 1841 to six and a half million in 1851.

19 The IRISH CONFEDERATION was founded on 13 January, 1847. It proclaimed the right of self-government to Ireland but disavowed the use of force or separation from England.

20 COERCION ACTS were passed at Westminster to give the Irish administration special emergency powers of repression. One hundred and five such Acts were passed between 1800 and December, 1921.

21 The UNITED IRISHMAN was founded by John Mitchel in 1847. It

advocated advanced republican views and despite its price of two shillings, sold five thousand copies of the first issue.

22 Quoted in T.A.JACKSON, Ireland Her Own. 1946. Page 238.

23 THE UNITED IRISHMAN, 26 January, 1848.

24 MICHAEL DOHNEY reached Manchester from Ireland in 1848. He played a prominent part in formulating the agreement between the Irish Confederates and the Chartists. He made an extensive speaking tour of Northern England. On his return to Dublin in July, 1848, he was arrested together with T.F.Meagher.

25 DOROTHY THOMPSON, The Chartists. (1948) Page 318.

26 WILLIAM SMITH O'BRIEN (1803–1864) was born in Ireland and educated at Harrow and Trinity College, Cambridge. He was elected to Parliament for Ennis from 1828–1841. He supported Daniel O'Connell's Catholic Association. He participated in the abortive rising in County Tipperary in 1848. He was captured and condemned to death but the sentence was commuted to transportation to Tasmania. He was released and returned to Ireland in 1854.

27 J.J. FINNIGAN Manchester Irishman and follower of Daniel O'Connell. In 1848 he was one of the militant Irish Confederates.

28 THOMAS FRANCIS MEAGHER (1822–1867) was born in Waterford and educated for the law. He worked as a journalist and supported YOUNG IRELAND, becoming a close friend of O'Brien and Mitchel. He was arrested for his part in the rising in Tipperary in 1848 and was sentenced to transportation to Tasmania. He escaped to the United States and during the Civil War, became Brigadier General of the New York Irish Brigade. He became Acting General of Montana from 1865–1866.

29 LEEDS TIMES. 8 April, 1848.

30 MECW. Vol.6. Page 447.

31 JOHN SAVILLE, 1848, The British State and the Chartist Movement. (1987) Page 127. (SAVILLE, 1848)

32 DOROTHY THOMPSON, The Chartist Experience. Pages 142/143

33 JOHN DENVIR, The Irish In Britain (1894) Page 140. COLONEL MACARONE's pamphlet Defensive Instructions For The People (1832) circulated widely among the physical force Chartists in a cheap 6d edition.

34 JOHN WEST (1811–1887) was born in Ireland and emigrated to England in the 1830s when the Irish textile industry collapsed. He worked as a hand – loom silk weaver in Macclesfield and became an eloquent and accomplished speaker strongly advocating repeal of the union. At the 1847 General Election, he was the Chartist candidate for Stockport and won decisively at the hustings. He was arrested and imprisoned several times. He died in poverty.

35 J.E.P. WALLIS. State Trials. Vol. 7 Page 737 (State Trials)

36 Quoted in SAVILLE, 1848. Page 114.

37 GEORGE ARCHDEACON was a prominent Liverpool Chartist.

38 EDWARD CLARK CROPPER, like many Chartists continued his political activity after 1848. He was elected as a delegate to the 1854

Labour Parliament convened by Ernest Jones in support of Preston strikers.

39 Miners had a tradition of industrial struggle for Chartist objectives. Many Miners' leaders were Chartists and WILLIAM GROCOTT, Secretary of the Lancashire Miners' Association was also Secretary of the South Lancashire Chartists. Chartism was a training ground for many who later became leaders of the miners.

40 Quoted in P.W. SLOSSON, The Decline of The Chartist Movement. (1976). Page 100.

41 SAVILLE, 1848. Page 143.

42 GEORGE WHITE (1812–1868) was an active radical and Chartist from the early 1830s until 1860. He was praised by George Jacob Holyoake as "frank, generous and brave." Born in Cork, he moved to Leicester as a young man and then worked as a woolcomber in Leeds. He was sent as a Chartist lecturer to many places. Imprisoned on several occasions, in 1849 when with WEST and LEACH in a cell, he wrote:
".. we are in a prison cast,
Apart from friends to dwell,
But stern resolve and dauntless mind,
And boundless love for human kind,
Still consecrates our cell"
S. ROBERTS, Politicians and Poets. (1993). Page 27.

43 SAVILLE, 1848. Page 150.

44 The treatment which was meted out to Jones was severe in the extreme. For 19 months he was in solitary confinement in a cell 13 feet by 6 feet. He was not allowed pen, paper or ink. He refused to degrade himself by picking oakum and thus earned a bread and water diet and the denial of anything to read, even the Bible. In spite of hardship, he wrote some of the finest poems in the English language and when denied the means to do so, he made an ink well from soap and used his own blood to write on any scrap of paper he could lay his hands on. He became extremely emaciated and ill. While he was in prison, his wife and family suffered extreme hardship and poverty.

45 SAVILLE, 1848. Pages 140–144.

46 SAVILLE, 1848. Page 153.

47 While he was trying to preserve order in Manchester in April, 1848, General Arbuthnot had to send a regiment to Ireland. In July when the insurrection led by Smith O'Brien broke out, three regiments were suddenly withdrawn from the Northern Command. These could only be replaced by bringing troops from distant places.

48 THE ENGLISH PATRIOT AND THE IRISH REPEALER printed and published by James Leach between 22 July and 2 December,1848.

49 GEORGE WEBBER (1823–1895) was a Halifax woolcomber. He was a Republican and physical force Chartist involved in 1848 in nightly armed drillings on Skircoat Moor. Arrested in Manchester with George White, he was sentenced to nine months in York Castle, but escaped while being

taken there. In the 1850s he was an active Co-operator and Secretary of the Halifax Branch of the Reform League.

50 SAMUEL McGOWAN KYDD (1815–1892) was born in Scotland and became a shoemaker and Chartist lecturer, writer and poet. From 1861 he practised as a barrister with Chambers in the Middle Temple. He was much in demand as a lecturer. He stood for Greenwich in the 1847 General Election, won on a show of hands and then withdrew from the poll. He was an ardent supporter of the Land Company. In 1848, he and James Leach travelled to Ireland to cement the alliance between the Chartists and the Confederates. After 1851, he played no further part in the Chartist Movement.

51 JOHN McCREA was a preacher and schoolmaster in Cumnock. He was active in the radical movement from 1819. In 1839 he was a delegate from Ayreshire to the General Convention of The Industrious Classes in Birmingham. He contested Greenock in the 1847 General Election as a Chartist candidate. He supported O'Connor and formed a National Guard in Dundee in 1848.

52 STICKFAST: THE SPY OF 1848. Pamphlet. 8 Pages. 1848.

53 STATE TRIALS. Page 747.

54 STATE TRIALS. Page 794.

55 WILLIAM GROCOTT was a Manchester weaver who became Secretary of the Lancashire Miners' Association in 1843. In 1847 he became Secretary of the Miners' Association of Great Britain and Ireland which gave strong support to the NCA.

56 THOMAS RANKIN (1821–?) was a Salford Chartist lecturer and engraver. He played a major part in a strike of building workers in 1846 which led to a meeting of Manchester Trades, Rankin played a prominent part in the proceedings.

57 J.EPSTEIN and D.THOMPSON, The Chartist Experience. (1982) Page 299.

58 HARNEY PAPERS. edited by Frank and Renee Black, (1969) Page 83.

59 Chartist Tracts For The Times
No.1. not traced
No.2. Why Are We Poor? The Landed Aristocracy;
No.4. The Factory System; Trades' Union Strikes; the Operatives' Remedy.
No.5. What is Liberty? How Shall We Obtain it?
No.6. Home Colonisation! Liberty Further Defined!
No.7. Chartism and The Charter Defended.
Advertised in No.6 but not traced.
Wortley, Nr Leeds, (1848–1850)
Bibliography Of The Chartist Movement

Chapter Ten
Chartism in the 1850s

Fling out the Red Banner! the patriots perish!
But where their bones moulder the seed taketh root –
Their heart's-life ran red the great harvest to cherish,
Then gather ye Reapers, and garner the fruit.

Gerald Massey[1]

The thirties and forties, were a consciousness raising period when the workers became aware of their identity as a class, of their potential power in unity and their political responsibilities. The rate at which they were exploited helped to form their awareness and their determination to change their conditions. Those years were the training ground for the developments which followed. Technology which had overlapped with outdated industrial processes gained the upper hand and was accepted. Britain, for a time, was dominant in the world market and opportunities for employment increased. For example, cotton textiles and coal exports increased five times between 1850 and 1872.

Organisation on a class basis rested with the skilled craftsmen in their Trade Unions. Women and unskilled men remained mainly unorganised. The change in atmosphere was noted by Thomas Cooper who visited Manchester in 1850. He said:- "In our old Chartist time, it is true, Lancashire working men were in rags by thousands; and many of them often lacked food. But their intelligence was demonstrated wherever you went. You would see them

Thomas Cooper

in groups discussing the great doctrine of political justice – that every grown-up, sane man ought to have a vote in the election of the men who were to make the laws by which he was to be governed; or they were in earnest dispute respecting the teachings of Socialism. Now, you will see no such groups in Lancashire."[2] He noted that greyhounds, Building Society shares and pigeon racing had replaced democracy and socialism as topics of interest. The Corn Laws were gone and some factory reform had been achieved. Capitalism had found easier fields of exploitation in the Colonies. The workers in Britain had been appeased to some extent by some amelioration of their gross exploitation.

The Chartist ranks were depleted by repression, emigration and disillusionment and the changed economic situation affected their outlook. In February, 1850, Manchester membership of the NCA was reduced to about three hundred, a tenth of the previous decade. In 1839, most workshops and Trade Unions recognised the People's Charter. In 1850, it was the reverse. Manchester Chartists split. The majority, led by Daniel Donovan and James Leach, favoured an alliance between the workers and the middle class. The Parliamentary and Financial Reform Society gained strength in Lancashire. Formed in 1848 by Parliamentary Radicals, it advocated financial reform and the extension of the franchise to ratepayers. A Manchester Branch was formed by Abel Heywood and James Schofield and it rapidly gained the support of the majority of the Chartists.

Cooper was not the only observer to notice changes in the outlook of former revolutionaries. Returning to Manchester early in the fifties Frederick Engels was struck by the fundamental changes that had taken place. His "philistine" and business friends remained the same, but the two men whom he had considered to be nearest to him in political awareness, James Leach and John Watts, had radically changed their policy and political stance.

But there were those who retained their political awareness and followed Ernest Jones and George Julian Harney in a demand for "The Charter and Something More". The "more" increased as Socialism became recognised as the aim of the working class. This was developed after the publication of THE COMMUNIST

MANIFESTO in 1848. Harney had kept the Movement alive during Jones' imprisonment. But as soon as he was released, Jones outlined his assessment of the situation, In Harney's RED REPUBLICAN,[3] he wrote, "Chartism in 1850 is a different thing from Chartism in 1840. The leaders of the English Proletarians have proved that they are true Democrats, and no shams, by going ahead so rapidly within the last few years. They have progressed from the idea of a simple political reform to the idea of a Social Revolution."[4] In another issue he referred to Chartism under the Red Flag as being, "a vindication of the claims of labour."[5]

Under the influence of Jones and Harney, the NCA adopted a comprehensive programme of working class political, social and economic demands which laid the basis for modern Socialism. Ernest Jones recognised the importance of the theoretical work which Karl Marx and Frederick Engels were involved in and he kept in close touch with them. He understood the class nature of society and endeavoured to guide the Chartist Movement along lines which would enable it to play a significant part in developments. He said:-
The Capitalists of all kinds will be our foes as long as they exist, and carry on against us a war to the very knife. Therefore they must be put down. Therefore we must have class against class – that is, all the oppressed on one side, all the oppressors on the other. An amalgamation of classes is impossible where an amalgamation of interests is also impossible. CLASS AGAINST CLASS – all other mode of proceeding is mere moonshine."[6]

The Hall of Science had become Manchester Free Library, purchased with funds subscribed by a public appeal. John Watts was the broker who organised the deal. Engels wrote to Marx, "Watts is now on the best of terms with the Bishop of Manchester ... the fellow seems skilled in sharp practice and now has a much larger shop in Deansgate.[7] He has become a consummate radical mediocrity."[8] Engels sought out James Leach whom he had characterised as "honest, trustworthy and capable."[9] But found a considerable change in him also. At Ernest Jones' request, on 5 January, 1851, Engels attended a meeting at the People's Institute in Ancoats. The Manchester Chartist Council under the influence of Donovan and Leach called on it to advocate collaboration with the middle class on their terms. They offered Co-operative Societies as the answer to working class aspirations. Engels supported Jones who declared himself a Red Republican in favour of the nationalisation of landed property. Reporting to Marx, Engels wrote of Leach, "In spite of his disreputable atheism and socialism, the latter regards it as his vocation to acquire respectability in the eyes of the bourgeoisie."[10]

Engels was not the only one who was critical of Leach. Commenting on his support for Feargus O'Connor's Land Plan, Harney said, "Most of the owd chap's followers are poor ignorant blockheads. But Leach knows better. There is no man more thoroughly understands the real character of O'Connor."[11] Shortly after the January conference, Leach gave up all political activity to concentrate on earning a living.

On 17 May, 1852, a National Conference was held at the People's Institute with the aim of re-organising the movement. William Grocott and E. Clark Cropper represented Manchester and Salford. It was in session for five days and elected an Executive Committee consisting of R.G.Gammage,[12] James Finlen[13] and Ernest Jones with William Grocott as Secretary

In 1853, the PEOPLE'S PAPER[14] reported that there was a revival of interest in Manchester but that attendance at meetings was small. In April, 1854, Ernest Jones put forward the concept of a LABOUR PARLIAMENT in the paper. A Mass Movement Committee was formed with Edward Hoosen as Secretary.[15] The Labour Parliament met in the People's Institute from 6–18 March, 1854. There were about forty delegates present representing trade unions, towns and districts. Of the four from Manchester, only two had any previous connection with Chartism. The conference was preoccupied with the widespread industrial strife although political reform also had a place on the agenda. In spite of Marx's optimistic assessment of the conference, it produced no lasting results.

In 1855 a further attempt was made to revive Manchester Chartism. A meeting was called in Stevenon's Square which attracted about six hundred people, but it failed to make any organisational plans.

At the last NCA Conference in London in 1858, Manchester was represented by Edward Hoosen.[15] A policy of co-operation with the middle classes was accepted and Chartism as a militant organised mass movement was ended.

As Feargus O'Connor dominated the forties, Ernest Jones was the mainspring of the fifties He tramped the country spreading the gospel of organisation. He said in his first speech in Manchester after his release, "Two years ago, and more, I went to prison for speaking three words. Those words were; 'Organise – Organise – Organise' And now after two years and more of incarceration, I come forward again to raise that talismanic watchword of salvation – and this day again I say, 'ORGANISE! ORGANISE! ORGANISE'."[16]

The last manifestation of a mass movement was in Manchester and Salford on the occasion of Ernest Jones' funeral on Saturday 30 January, 1869 on a bleak winter's day. A huge crowd assembled outside his home in Wellington Street, Higher Broughton. At a quarter past three, the cortege set out for Ardwick Cemetery and gathering numbers from the huge crowds which lined the streets through which it passed took until 5 p.m. to reach its destination. There, Edward Beales, Secretary of the Reform League delivered the funeral oration. He said that Jones had combined "the erudition of a scholar, the genius of a poet, the fervent eloquence of the orator and the courageous and fervent spirit of the undaunted patriot who no persecution could frighten from the advocacy of his principles, whilst no temptation or threatened loss of fortune could tempt him to betray them."[17]

Jones died a poor man like so many of those who suffered as he had in the cause. In his case, a fund was opened to help support his widow and three children.

Notes

1 GERALD MASSEY (1828–1907) Song Of The Red Republican.
2 THOMAS COOPER, The Life Of Thomas Cooper (1872) Leicester (1971). pp.393/4.
3 RED REPUBLICAN 22 June, 1850 – 30 November, 1850.
4 RED REPUBLICAN, 22 June, 1850.
5 RED REPUBLICAN, 13 July, 1850.
6 NOTES TO THE PEOPLE. Vol.1 Page 342.
7 This shop was at 80 Deansgate according to the TRADES ADVOCATE

AND HERALD OF PROGRESS, a paper edited by John Watts for the iron trades. It was a weekly aimed at promoting amalgamation of the unions involved in the engineering industry. It ran from June to December, 1850.

8 MECW Vol 38. Page 255.

9 MECW Vol.3 Page 450.

10 MECW. Vol 38 Pages 63/64.

11 The Harney Papers edited by Frank and Renee Black. 1969. Page 83.

12 ROBERT GEORGE GAMMAGE 1815–1888) Historian of the Chartist Movement. Served apprenticeship as a coach-trimmer. Activist from age of seventeen. Chartist lecturer and later a shoemaker. Elected to NCA Executive, 1852. Was friend of Ernest Jones until 1853. Became medical doctor joining Royal College of Surgeons 1864. Practiced in Sunderland. Wrote numerous works on medicine.

13 JAMES FINLEN worked closely with Ernest Jones. In 1852 he and R.G. Gammage toured the country lecturing for the Chartists.

14 PEOPLE'S PAPER, 8 May, 1852 – June, 1858.

15 EDWARD HOOSEN (1825–1869) worked closely with Ernest Jones until the Chartist Conference in February, 1858 when he changed his policy and advocated co-operation with the middle class. He led the Reform Movement in South Lancashire in the sixties together with Abel Heywood.

16 NORTHERN STAR.26 October, 1850.

17 EDMUND BEALES. Address given at the funeral in Ardwick Cemetery, 30 January, 1869.

Chapter Eleven
Conclusion

With their faces to danger, like freemen they fought,
With their daring all heart and hand!
And the thunder-deed followed the lightening-thought
When they stood for their own good land

Gerald Massey[1]

Chartism was the adolescence of the labour movement. It developed in response to the acute exploitation of capitalism in its expanding stages. It marked the understanding by workers that they were a class in society with power and a responsibility to use it to improve their conditions. The strike in 1842 was a landmark in that consciousness. But unfortunately they were unable to use their power effectively because at that stage they were unclear whom they were opposing. Locally, the pattern of economic struggle against employers was obvious, but translating that into politics with an understanding that social evils cannot be abolished until the forces supporting the situation – the Monarchy, privilege and wealth are also ended is more complicated.

The people's Charter was not an answer to the social evils. It certainly laid the basis for future developments which led to some social changes. But social evils need to be studied and understood and that, the workers had not, at that stage, been able to do. It was only after Karl Marx and Frederick Engels formulated Scientific Socialism that theoretical clarity became possible. Ernest Jones began the task of guiding Chartists along the right lines. However, Chartism was not a socialist movement. It was only a radical democratic movement. Although their social aims were implicit, they were not formulated as a socialist programme. THE CHARTER AND SOMETHING MORE indicated the underlying understanding that enfranchisement would not, of itself, solve the social evils.

At a reunion of old Chartists held in Manchester Reform club in 1898, the veterans were welcomed by the Chairman who said that it required great courage, resolution, determination and insensibility to consequences, to alter the state of things and that was the merit which belonged to the Chartists. The Charter, he said, "had given the people a voice ... it had given the people a sense of power which, when the sense of unity came into their minds, would make them an effective power in the State. It was something to belong to such a movement. A man might die with pride in the consciousness that the class to which he belonged possessed the power, and that he assisted to confer it."[2] Replying to the welcome, George Jacob Holyoake spoke of the dreams of the Chartists. When the poor toiled like slaves, languished in wretchedness and were nothing in the State, it had been their dream to change that situation. Their object had been to make people an effective power in the State. The merit of the Charter was that it claimed that people should have a voice in governing themselves.

To that extent, Chartism failed. Capitalism was too strong and was still developing. The working class was immature, unsure of its future and divided in its leadership. At crucial times, their vacillations and confusions led to defeat. It took another forty years for an independent working class movement to take its place in the political life of the country and during that time, ex-Chartists were active in many different spheres using their experience and knowledge to build the basis on which it was founded. The Trade Unions, the Co-operative Movement, the Women's Franchise struggles, Friendly Societies and small local groups too numerous to mention benefitted from participation of those who had won their spurs in the Chartist years.

The achievement of Chartism has never been lost. The

outpouring of academic work based on the twenty years of its activity show how deeply its roots penetrated. Many of the lessons of the Chartist era have yet to be learned by modern workers who need to articulate their aims and identify their enemy in the same way that their ancestors struggled to do over a century ago. The methods of struggle through education and the development of culture are as relevant today as they were then.

It is perhaps less easy in our highly developed technological age to identify coherent aims. But as George Julian Harney said in 1848 "those who till the soil shall be its masters; and those who raise the food shall be its first partakers; that those who build mansions shall live in them... that none but the idle shall die of hunger, and none but the vicious suffer reproach." Fundamentally we cannot quarrel with him. The world is more complex. But our responsibility must be to pass on the heritage of struggle and determination to end exploitation that the Chartists initiated.

Manchester and Salford were the focal points of the Chartist Movement last century. As the millennium approaches, maybe the workers in the modern cities can play a similar rôle in articulating and developing a socialist movement that will bring what the Chartists really wanted – to change the world so that all can live in peace and with dignity. Ernest Jones' dreams are our dreams.

> Dreams
> Are but the light of clearer skies –
> Too dazzling for our naked eyes.
> And when we catch their flashing beams,
> We turn aside and call them dreams.
> Oh, trust me, every thought that yet
> In greatness rose and sorrow set,
> That Time to ripening glory nurst,
> Was called an "idle dream" at first.[3]

Notes

1 A Red Republican Lyric. JUSTICE, 1 November, 1884.

2 Locomotive Engineers and Firemen's Journal Vol 11 No. 12 December 1898 Pages 547–549.

3 ERNEST JONES, The Painter of Florence. in NOTES TO THE PEOPLE No.1 Page 44.

Further Reading

PAUL A. PICKERING: Chartism and the Chartists in Manchester and Salford. ISBN 0-333-62052-6. Macmillan Press Ltd 1995.

JOHN SAVILLE: 1848, The British State and The Chartist Movement. ISBN 0 521 33341 5. Cambridge University Press. 1987.

MICK JENKINS: The General Strike of 1842. ISBN 85315 488 0. Lawrence and Wishart. 1980.

STEPHEN ROBERTS: Radical Politicians and Poets In Early Victorian Britain. ISBN 0-7734-9126-0. Studies In British History Vol. 27. Edwin Mellen Press.

FREDERICK ENGELS: The Condition Of The Working Class In England From Personal Observation and Authentic Sources. ISBN 0 85315-294-2.

KARL MARX AND FREDERICK ENGELS 1844–1845. Collected Works. Vol.4. Lawrence and Wishart. 1975.

Index